More praise for *The Modern Dad's Dilemma* and the work of John Badalament

"What I find especially inspiring about John is how much he gets the dilemma of the average guy who craves connection to his own father or child but who lacks the skills — or the social permission — to do anything about it."

— Jackson Katz, PhD, author of *The Macho Paradox: Why Some Men Hurt Women and How All Men Can Help*

"John's ability to connect and convey his message to parents and professionals is superb. All parents, both mothers and fathers alike, should hear what John Badalament has to say about what our children need to hear."

— Janis Santos, National Head Start Association board of directors

"Every wife will want her husband to read this book. *The Modern Dad's Dilemma* is a much-needed tool that enables men to become the kind of father they wish to be."

— Tamara Monosoff, author of *Secrets of Millionaire Moms*

"Don't miss any opportunity to hear him speak."

— William Pollack, assistant clinical professor of psychiatry at Harvard University and author of *Real Boys*

"John Badalament has given modern dads a Mapquest to family harmony. These exercises will absolutely take you to a place of parental integrity."

— Haji Shearer, director of the Fatherhood Initiative at the Massachusetts Children's Trust Fund

"In my work as a counselor over the past twenty-five years, it has been easy to see the impact of father absence — physically and emotionally — on the lives of their children. In my role as a father of two young boys it has been humbling to come to terms with my own absence and a challenge not to deny it. John Badalament's book is more than a wake-up call for fathers like me; it is precisely the type of support I need to show up for my children and to remain present in all the ways that are so vitally necessary — for them, for our family, and for me."

— Dr. Michael J. Nakkula, assistant professor at the Harvard Graduate School of Education and coauthor of *Understanding Youth*

THE
MODERN
DAD'S
DILEMMA

THE MODERN DAD'S DILEMMA

HOW TO STAY CONNECTED WITH YOUR KIDS IN A RAPIDLY CHANGING WORLD

JOHN BADALAMENT, EDM

New World Library
Novato, California

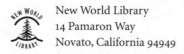

New World Library
14 Pamaron Way
Novato, California 94949

Text design by Mary Ann Casler and John Aldrich

Library of Congress Cataloging-in-Publication Data
Badalament, John.
The modern dad's dilemma : how to stay connected with your kids in a rapidly changing world / John Badalament.
    p.   cm.
Includes bibliographical references and index.
ISBN 978-1-57731-660-2 (pbk. : alk: paper)
1. Fathers. 2. Father and child. 3. Families. I. Title.
HQ756.B33 2010
306.874'2—dc22   2010001719

First printing, April 2010
ISBN 978-1-57731-660-2
Printed in Canada on 100% postconsumer-waste recycled paper

 New World Library is a proud member of the Green Press Initiative.

10 9 8 7 6 5 4 3 2 1

This book is dedicated to my family:

to Stella, my star;
to bighearted Jake;
to my beautiful wife, Katie;

to my mother, Diane McManus Jensen;
my stepfather, David Jensen;
and my father, Tony Badalament.

Contents

Introduction

At the age of twenty-five, not yet a dad myself, I walked into my father's office to reconcile our past — he thought we were going out for lunch. Up until that point I had not yet discovered the courage to speak honestly and directly with my father about the past. All that would change in just ten short minutes.

I told my father that we weren't actually going to lunch, that he should stay seated and not respond to anything he was about to hear. He had been given plenty of time to speak over the years; now it was my turn to talk. Barely able to breathe, I said, "You've done a lot of great things for me as a dad." After describing a few, such as how he had supported my love of baseball and patiently taught me how to drive, I said, "And . . . I want you to know that growing up with you was also very, very difficult. You were irresponsible, alcoholic, and abusive. As a consequence, I have struggled, and still struggle to this day, to feel good about myself. I don't want you to do anything. I'm an adult, and these are my issues to deal with now."

He opened his mouth to speak, and for the first time ever, I raised my hand and without a word, motioned for him to stop. I knew that if I allowed him to talk, he would almost certainly try to explain, minimize, or deny what I was saying, and like most loyal sons, I would back down from speaking the truth of my experience.

Confronting my father at the age of twenty-five was the single most difficult, emotionally raw moment of my life. As a kid, I was taught that vulnerability got you nothing but trouble and thus learned to hate it. The currency of my upper-middle-class boyhood was as follows: being tough, "getting" the girls, and holding your own in sports. If you had no currency, you were at risk of verbal or physical reprisals. I spent a great deal of time and energy avoiding situations in which I could be taken advantage of, proved wrong, or made to look like a "wimp." Implicitly, discussing feelings and relationships with or around other boys was forbidden.

When I left my dad's office that day, I assumed my departure would mark the end of our relationship, that he would want nothing more to do with me. Paradoxically, once I found my voice and spoke up — as uncomfortable and frightening as it was — our relationship actually grew stronger. While we didn't necessarily spend more time together, speak more often, or agree on everything (past or present), a more honest dialogue developed between us. There was no longer one voice, one truth, or one authority. We became two adults, not a father and a child. Don't get me wrong; my dad didn't enjoy the experience of being confronted with his past, but the effect of that one conversation was deep and long-lasting.

Four years ago my father became ill from years of neglecting his diabetes. As his condition worsened, it became clear he wouldn't be leaving the hospital. I remember looking him in the eye one afternoon and saying, "You can go now, Dad. There's nothing left to do here." He looked back at me, smiled, teared up, and nodded. Our peace was made. A few days later he quietly passed away.

I feel fortunate for having had the chance to reconcile with him — by holding my father lovingly accountable, as each new generation must do — but sad that so much of his story was shrouded in mystery. I knew very little about his life as a husband and a dad: What did he love about being a husband and a father? What did he worry about as a father? What brought him joy? When did he feel like he was doing a great job as a father? What did marriage and fatherhood mean to him?

It's never too late for the truth. This is why I remind dads — myself included — of that all-too-common movie scene in which the dad is on his deathbed and finally tries to talk to his adult child (usually a son) to admit his mistakes, to reveal his humanity, thereby giving the purest possible expression of love. Finally, in the fading light, his vulnerability opens the door for the child to have a voice, to reconcile a lifetime of distance, conflict, absence, or emotional silence. As modern dads, we must rewrite this scene for our children. They need not wait so long.

In my educational consulting work, I do an activity with students in which they anonymously write down two questions they've always wanted to ask their dad. No matter what their ethnic, cultural, racial, or socioeconomic background is, the students' two most common questions are almost always: "What was your relationship like with your father?" and "What was your childhood like?" (sometimes worded as, "What were you like at my age?"). Though they may not ask, children want and need their dad's stories, even if they never knew who their dad was. I call it the elephant in the living room of child development: the missing stories of men's lives, particularly men's emotional lives.

Like many dads, growing up I did not have the kind of close, emotionally connected relationship with my father that I want with my children today. Are there aspects of his legacy I want to keep or pass

on to my children? Yes. Are there mistakes I'm determined not to repeat? Of course. This is not, however, a matter of intention only —
what dad doesn't *want* to be close with his children? The question
is *how*: How can I give what I didn't get?

In my workshops for parents, I often ask dads to describe the
kind of relationship they are trying to build with their children.
Whether I'm at an elite private school, a prison, or a public library,
the responses are similar. Most dads and dad figures want to have a
strong, close bond with their children, to always be a trustworthy
and vital presence, and to be someone to turn to for advice, support,
or just to talk with. Most dads want their sons and daughters to feel
secure in knowing that they can always come to them and share
what's going on in their lives, good and bad.

In the past decade of working with dads of all backgrounds, I
have heard this chorus grow louder: modern dads want connection,
closeness, and intimacy. Unlike fathers of generations past, whose
lives were so often cloaked in silence and mystery, dads today are increasingly vocal about this vision. Modern dads want to be the competent, caring, and supportive parents and partners that deep down
we know we are capable of becoming. This is my cause for hope.

It starts with modern dads speaking the truth about what fatherhood means to us — how it challenges our beliefs about manhood, raises fears about repeating mistakes of the past, and ultimately
reveals our capacity to love another human being unconditionally.
It starts with also making space in our relationships to truly listen
to our loved ones. Our children and families not only want but need
us to deliver on this new vision of fatherhood.

Three essential qualities are vital in realizing this new vision:

1. *Self-knowledge.* A modern dad envisions a healthy future for his
kids by understanding his past.

Where did you learn to be a father? Who are your models?

What does a successful, healthy, and solid relationship look like? How will you pass on the gifts from your father's legacy, while protecting your children from the mistakes? Being clear about the quality of relationship you want with your children — and about how to go about achieving that — is critical; to do so without an honest look at your own positive and negative experiences growing up with (or without) your father, mother, and other caregivers is a mistake.

One factor that heavily influences everything we do as parents — yet one we're rarely even aware of — is our belief system. What you believe about women, children, fatherhood, parenting, and manhood is rooted in your past and plays out in your present. Your family structure (whether your parents are divorced, whether you were adopted, whether you have siblings), racial-ethnic identity, class background, religion, neighborhood all enter into this. For example, a friend of mine — who also happens to have performed a few root canals in my mouth — Dr. Fardad Mobed, forty-nine, was raised in a traditional Iranian household in which the children (both sons) were meant to be seen, not heard. As a modern dad in America, not only does Dr. Mobed want his daughter (now three) to feel listened to, but he also hopes she'll always feel comfortable opening up to him. At the same time he says, "There are things I don't want to know about, conversations better left for her mother." Dr. Mobed's belief system about raising his daughter is complex, formed as much by his experience of cultural norms in Iranian society as by his experience of raising a girl in contemporary American society. Without exploring the past, he may simply have treated his daughter as he was treated and as he saw girls treated in Iran.

2. *Courage.* A modern dad has the courage to explore different ways of fathering — even if it means failing, not having all the answers, or appearing "unmanly."

Stepping into the unfamiliar or the unknown takes courage. For a guy like Dr. Mobed, it is a small act of courage every time he listens to — and doesn't fix, dismiss, or ignore — his daughter (or wife) describe a problem. For another dad, it is a small act of courage to proactively get involved in making doctor appointments, arranging childcare, or joining the PTA at his son's school. And for many dads, just getting down on the floor, being present, and playing with their kids takes courage. As with the first stay-at-home dads who pushed baby strollers into a playground full of mothers — and undoubtedly got looks that said, "Why isn't he working" or "What's wrong with him?" — it takes courage to go against what you have seen around you, to speak or act in ways that feel uncomfortable, and to step into a role that is new and not yet defined.

Is the bar that low? Do these seemingly trite changes constitute acts of courage? Haven't we seen the "new father" or the "sensitive dad" before? The answer to all these questions is yes — with one major caveat. Never before have men begun to embrace the qualities of caretaking at a time when women are closer than ever to the ideal of equality.

3. *Adaptability.* A modern dad sees the rapidly changing roles of men in family life as an opportunity — not a burden — to be a better dad.

In any time of great social change, there is always a sense of confusion, uncertainty, or even chaos. As women have collectively worked to redefine womanhood and motherhood over decades (especially in the latter half of the twentieth century), the very foundations of traditional, patriarchal society — white men assuming the exclusive right to power and privilege, while subordinating and subjugating women, people of color, and other groups — have begun to shake. The civil rights movement, the gay and lesbian rights movement, and the women's movement have all contributed to the current reconfiguring of modern fatherhood and masculinity.

Although the gender wars continue to rage, fundamentally women's progress (along with the economic reality that surviving on one income has become increasingly difficult in contemporary America) has changed the rules of the game for everyone, especially dads. Breadwinning and the working world are no longer the exclusive domains of men. This has left dads with a critical choice: embrace, or at the very least accept, change or rail against it. Do we see the emerging job description of fatherhood — which involves tasks and roles more closely associated to stereotypical "women's work," such as cleaning and childcare — as an opportunity to be better dads, capable of raising healthy, strong, and bighearted girls and boys? Or do we see modern fatherhood as a temporary setback to the natural order of things and long for the days when gender roles were more rigidly defined?

Over the past ten years I've spoken to thousands of fathers across the country and abroad, and I've researched, written, and made a documentary film about what it means to be a modern dad. The dilemma I consistently hear is this: How do I build and maintain a strong, emotionally connected relationship with my kids *and* get to work by 8 AM? In other words, how do I become a breadwinner *and* a caretaker?

Whether it means leaving work early to attend their child's game or play, staying up late with a sick child, talking through a relationship problem with a partner, or attending a parent-teacher conference at school, many modern dads are determined to show up for our families in ways our own fathers could or did not. However, we're also just discovering what most mothers have known for years: doing it all isn't easy. It's especially difficult when you don't have many role models to follow.

Women have traveled a great distance on the road from house-wife to working woman. They are not turning around. Now is the time for us as dads to ask more of ourselves. Being a father is not something you are; it's something you *do*. By showing up for our children and partners, learning new skills, building support networks, and measuring success by the quality and health of our relationships, modern dads have only just set out on the road leading back home.

My goal is for this book to serve as your road map on your journey. It is also intended to serve as the bridge between the legacy we carry from the past and the emerging vision of fatherhood.

About This Book

Personally and professionally, as an educator and counselor, I have seen the tremendous impact fathers, present and absent, have on their children. In an effort to raise awareness and spark dialogue about this subject, I created a documentary film, *All Men Are Sons: Exploring the Legacy of Fatherhood*. The film follows the lives of five men from diverse backgrounds as each explores his father's legacy; it initially aired on PBS in 2002. Since then, I have been lecturing about fatherhood to parent groups in schools, companies, community organizations, therapists, corrections facilities, and others across the country.

The initial response to the lectures surprised me. I was warned not to expect many dads to show up, that the crowd would be mostly women. The opposite was true. Men have consistently outnumbered women at most of my lectures. And not only did dads show up — they engaged in substantive discussions.

Inspired by these conversations and themes, I created Dialogues with Dad, a workshop (and retreat) bringing dads and sons, and dads and daughters, together to strengthen their relationships. The concept was simple: get dads and children in the same room, share stories about important topics, teach them how to talk and listen to each other skillfully, and coach them on how to keep the connection going. The results were extraordinary.

A ten-year-old boy used one of the activities, "speaking assertively," to let his dad know how much his yelling frightened him. The dad, floored by his son's feedback, agreed to get it under control. After a dad-daughter workshop, a group of young girls said they'd "never seen men talk like that," referring to the stories dads told about their own boyhoods.

Consistently, dads and children left Dialogues with Dad feeling closer, better able to handle conflict, and more equipped to have regular heart-to-heart talks. For most, Dialogues with Dad was a much-needed tune-up; for some, it was the grease to keep their already solid relationship rolling; and for a few, it was a new beginning altogether.

After I had been speaking and leading workshops for years, the next question seemed obvious: Could I write a book that would combine the practicality from Dialogues with Dad with the information and spirited discussion from my lectures? Could a book capture the energy of a roomful of dads, provide key research in a digestible format, and teach usable skills? The answer to these questions is the book you hold in your hands.

The Modern Dad's Dilemma will provide you with the everyday stories of modern dads, as well as practical skills and activities to help you stay connected, both with your children and with your partner. It is written for all dads with children of all ages, whether you are married or single, cohabitating or living away from your kids, a stepdad, grandfather, or primary adult male caregiver. Depending on your situation, you may use the book in different ways:

- *For dads-to-be and dads with newborns, infants, or toddlers.* This book will help you craft a vision for the kind of relationship you want with your child and develop a foundation of relationship skills and habits.
- *For dads with school-aged children.* This book will help you keep the lines of communication open and your relationship strong as your children's interests, personalities, and priorities change.
- *For dads with teenagers and young adults.* This book will help you stay close without being intrusive, talk about critical issues, and chart a new course for your relationship as your child moves toward adulthood.
- *For moms and women.* This book will give you insight into the complex, rarely explored inner lives of everyday dads as well as practical activities you can pass on, suggest, or simply encourage the dads or dads-to-be in your life to use today.

I collected the stories in this book by interviewing dads and dad figures from a diversity of backgrounds across the country. Most of the men I had met at my workshops and lectures, some were referred to me by friends and colleagues, and others just seemed to appear. I also interviewed a few of the men's wives, partners, children, and fathers as a way of filling out their stories.

While the stories in this book range across racial and ethnic background, socioeconomic status, sexual orientation, religion, geography, ability, and age, what holds them all together is this: each of the dads featured in this book embodies some aspect of what I defined above as three essential qualities of a modern dad: self-knowledge, courage, and adaptability. Each dad is featured in at least one chapter; in some cases he may show up in more than one.

Chapter 1 asks you to look twenty years into the future and

imagine your child being interviewed about his or her relationship with you. You will be asked to create a Dad's Vision Statement, an activity designed to help you carve out your "mission statement" as a father.

Now that you have begun to map out your priorities as a dad, chapter 2 asks you to become the bridge between your past and future. It will provide you with a step-by-step process for exploring how your past affects your present life as a dad. Chapter 3 demonstrates how several dads are handling the radically changing expectations and job descriptions for fatherhood today. In this chapter you will also find an exercise designed to help you evaluate the division of labor (work in and outside the home, unpaid and paid) in your family.

Whereas chapter 3 will get you thinking about some of the issues facing modern dads, chapter 4 is geared more toward solutions. The first exercise in this chapter will give you the chance to explore your priorities and determine what needs realignment. The second part of the chapter focuses on the importance of building rituals into your daily life as a dad, and you will learn about how to create what I call Ritual Dad Time. Chapter 5 moves into the profound subject of forging an emotional connection with your child. You will be introduced to the concept of *knowing* and will learn why you need to become an expert on your children's inner and outer lives. The exercises in this chapter will help you develop your listening skills and provide you with ways to stay consistently tuned into to your children.

In chapter 6 you will see that connecting emotionally requires not only that we be experts about our children's lives — that we *know* them — but that we be willing and courageous enough to let down our guard and *be known*. By using the practical guidelines and story prompts, you will learn how making yourself known is essential to forging healthy connections and communication with your children. The chapter concludes with a powerful activity called the Modern Dad's Relationship Checkup, which brings these two aspects of emotional connection — knowing and being known — together. It is a practical, structured way for you and your children to talk consistently and honestly about the quality of your relationship. It also provides you both with a built-in mechanism for handling difficult conversations and having what I call "an ongoing heart-to-heart."

Finally, in the appendix you will find practical skill-building exercises to do by yourself, with your children, or with your partner. These are the same exercises — in their full form — that I gave to the dads featured in this book to do. These exercises are sequenced to build on each other. Viewed as a whole, they present a complete and clear vision for modern fatherhood.

Modern fatherhood is about devoting yourself to something or someone greater than yourself. I believe that modern fatherhood has great potential for redefining manhood so that it's less about the endless, illusory quest for power and privilege and more about the steadfast commitment to bringing ourselves more fully and equally into our relationships at home. Being a dedicated dad, a loving partner or husband, a faithful friend, and a committed family and community member requires courage unlike the kind we see depicted in action movies or television dramas. The root of the word *courage* is the French word *coeur*, or "heart." Courage is an inner strength, a strength of the heart. Sons and daughters need their dads' heart strength. Modern dads can and must show their own children, as well as those who don't have a dad in their lives, such courage.

Create Your Own Vision

Imagine that twenty years from now your child is being interviewed for a documentary film about your life. Now imagine that the filmmaker asks your child to describe his or her relationship with you," I said to the five dads sitting in front of me in a circle. "What do you hope your child will say in that interview?" In a larger circle of chairs surrounding us sat their sons and daughters, as well as about fifteen other dad-child pairs. They sat very still while the dads contemplated this simple, provocative question. One by one, each of the dads in the small circle looked up and responded. "I hope my daughter says, 'Dad always took the time to be with me.'" "I hope he says, 'Dad taught me how to respect women, how to be a good husband.'" "I hope he says, 'Dad talked to me; he was someone I could trust with anything.'"

Now with a captivated audience — children and dads alike — most of whom had never seen a group of adult men speak so honestly and openly, I asked a follow-up question: "What do you hope your child will *not* say in an interview about his or her relationship with you?" Again there was a pause, but this time there were smiles. "This one's not so hard, is it?" I said with a chuckle. As a dad myself, I know how quickly I can access my fears and insecurities about fathering. Then the dads answered: "I hope my son doesn't say, 'Thanks, Mom! Dad was never around.'" "I hope my daughter doesn't say, 'Dad wasn't somebody I could talk to.'" "I hope he doesn't say, 'Dad pushed me too hard.'" "I hope she doesn't say, 'Dad never listened to me.'"

After all five dads had spoken, I asked for a volunteer. Jeremy, a stocky dad in his late thirties with an eight-year-old-son, Kyle, agreed to be the guinea pig. He turned and scanned the outer circle of observers to find his son. Kyle flashed Jeremy a nervous smile and gave a quick nod of approval.

This last part, I explained, is where the rubber meets the road. Jeremy repeated his answer to the first question. Twenty years from now he hoped his son would say, "I feel really close to my dad. He was always there for me." "So, Jeremy," I asked, "what are you *currently doing to increase the odds* of your son actually saying such things in 2030?" Jumping right in, Jeremy described how he volunteers in Kyle's classroom at school, how he constantly plays sports with him, and how much one-on-one time they spend together. The other dads nodded, seemingly impressed with his answer. Kyle had a grin plastered on his face. Following up, I asked what he will do in the future to keep the odds favorable. "I guess I've got to figure out what I'm going to do when he's a teenager and doesn't want me around so much." Jeremy was clearly involved in Kyle's life and had a sense of the challenges ahead.

We moved on to another question. "I hope Kyle wouldn't say, 'Dad was too hard on me' or 'he didn't let me be myself,'" Jeremy said somewhat sheepishly. Whenever a dad speaks so honestly, especially with his child bearing witness, everyone else in the room seems to feel it. I paused for a few beats and then continued. "Is there anything you need to change, Jeremy, so that in twenty years Kyle won't say you were too hard on him?" I repeated the question. Then, as if admitting it to himself for the first time — let alone admitting it to his son — Jeremy said, "I need to stop pressuring him, and stop worrying that he won't be interested in sports." He sighed, as if a big weight had been lifted, and turned to Kyle.

I continued, "Finally, what are your priorities from this moment forward?" Almost before I could finish my sentence, Jeremy said, "I'm going to tell him a story about the pressure I felt to be a star athlete, and I'm going to pay more attention to him, to what he's interested in."

"Sounds like a plan," I said. Kyle was beaming.

Your Dad's Vision Statement

In the story above, each of the five dads, Jeremy in particular, began to create what I call a Dad's Vision Statement. Whether it's for a Fortune 500 company, a global relief agency, or a personal relationship, an effective vision statement clarifies a sense of purpose, priorities, and values. Part of the Red Cross's mission is "to provide relief to victims of disaster." The purpose is helping those in great need, the focus is on victims of disaster, and the inherent values are, among many, compassion and care. We can see from Jeremy's story above that his purpose is to have a close relationship with his son, that his priorities are being involved and present, and that he values attention, listening, and growth.

Creating a Dad's Vision Statement will help you clarify your sense of purpose as a dad and guide you in important decisions. As the saying goes, "If you stand for nothing, you fall for anything." Without a vision, it's easy to get into the habit of being passive, of letting your circumstances or comfort level determine your course of action. As a new dad, I had ample opportunity to slide into the role of passive dad from the very start. I discovered, for example, that the world-class hospital where our daughter would be born offered exactly zero classes or groups geared toward dads. In the maternity ward, many of the important instructions about our baby were directed at my wife. By the time we returned home, the disparity in how competent I felt as a caregiver and how competent my wife, Katie, felt was large and growing. It was then that my vision of being an involved, capable, and nurturing dad began to crystallize. Only weeks later, that vision guided me in making a decision that, ultimately, would have profound implications: instead of going with what seemed like a default arrangement, in which I would go back to work full-time and Katie would stay home with Stella, we decided to split the childcare and each work part-time. Both of us would get equal time in and out of our comfort zones. Katie stepped out of her comfort zone each morning that she had to leave for work, watching me pack the diaper bag. And I stepped out of mine when, instead of heading off to work, I prepared my daughter for an outing to the park.

With a vision to guide one's decisions and actions as a dad, it's also easier to become more *proactive* and less *reactive*. This is especially true when children enter adolescence. Last spring I met a dad, Ron, whose stepson, Warren, was in his last year of elementary school. In his Dad's Vision Statement Ron wrote about his commitment to open, honest communication with Warren, despite claiming not to understand the world of teenagers today. Ron was contemplating his concerns over his stepson moving to a much larger middle school in a matter of months, and his vision statement helped clarify a key priority: "I will make sure to talk with Warren about the big issues — drugs and alcohol, peer pressure, sex, and dating — by the end of this school year." Without the awareness and focus of his vision statement, Ron said, he may have *thought* about talking with him, but more than likely he would have convinced himself it was unnecessary or, at best, he would have reminded Warren's mother to talk with him. Instead of being reactive and waiting to have his first discussion about alcohol with Warren the morning *after* he'd come home drunk, by using his vision statement, Ron was able to take a more preventive, proactive approach.

The Dad's Vision Statement is meant to serve as a living document. As you and your children grow and enter new stages of life, revisiting your vision can lead to a shift in priorities and a change in action. Recently, for example, my vision statement proved very useful in helping me make sense of a recurring conflict I was having with my five-year-old daughter. Under the guise of "not wanting her to be so shy," I found myself pushing Stella to be more outgoing and social, which, of course, she resisted. It felt like a lose-lose situation. The day after one such incident, in which I badgered her to leave my side at a birthday party and join the other girls her age, I decided to take a look at my Dad's Vision Statement.

The first line read, "I hope Stella says she felt loved and respected for being herself." This seemed pretty cut-and-dried. In this case, respecting Stella would mean I would have to stop pushing her. What, I wondered, could be so hard about that? As I dug a little deeper, I realized I had created a story in my head about her shyness: I was afraid that her shyness would lead to her becoming a follower, in turn making her more vulnerable and impressionable, which could lead to her getting taken advantage of or teased, which could lead to her falling in with the wrong crowd.... This far-fetched story, while possible, had actually blinded me to seeing, let alone respecting, Stella for "being herself."

From that one sentence in my Dad's Vision Statement, I was able to see the discrepancy between my intention and my actions. As I changed my behavior and let Stella be as shy as she needed to be, I gradually started seeing her in a completely different light: as a perceptive little girl who, in most social settings, likes to get the lay of the land — observe people, check out her surroundings — before diving in. And sometimes I still encourage Stella to take social risks. When she pushes back, however, I don't feel worried or frustrated. Instead, I've come to trust and genuinely admire her sense of knowing what she needs and who she is.

Having a vision for the relationship I want to build with my daughter was helpful in two ways. First, it served as a reminder that when a conflict persists, it's useful to step back and reflect on my motivations. So often when we butt heads or get into power struggles with our children, we forget to ask ourselves simple questions like, "Why am I taking this particular position?" or "Why does this issue continue to bother me so much?" Second, once I was able to see the forest for the trees, my vision statement made it abundantly clear what I needed to do — which, in this case, was to let go of trying to "make" my daughter into someone she's not.

The following story illustrates one modern dad's process of creating and using the Dad's Vision Statement in his everyday life. The kind of relationship Chris envisions with his daughter — trusting, open, supportive, caring — is shared by many dads who have done this activity. What I found so unique and important about his story, however, is his thoughtful, practical, and realistic approach to realizing his vision.

Chris Garniewicz, 39

FAMILY: married to Larah; father of a daughter, eight
BORN IN: Chelsea, Massachusetts
LIVES IN: Bluffton, South Carolina
OCCUPATION: professional firefighter and EMT, founder
   of Garniewicz Designs/The Art of Fire (custom-
   painted and sculpted helmet fronts and artwork on
   fire-related gear and equipment)

I met Chris three years ago after giving a talk to a room full of dads at his daughter's school in South Carolina. After just a few minutes of listening to Chris tell me about his relationship with his daughter, Hayden, I remember, I thought to myself, "This guy would be great to interview for the book," which at the time was in its formative stages. He posed a question: How do I come home from a job that essentially requires me to disconnect from my emotions and then try to be emotionally present for my daughter? The very nature of his question, as well as the discussion that followed, left me with a strong impression that Chris was not only interesting — he enjoys sewing with his daughter — but insightful, engaged, and actively trying to learn new and different ways of fathering.

While I left our conversation wanting to know more about his story, I had no doubt that Chris was a dad with a clear vision of the kind of relationship he wanted with his daughter. My hunch was confirmed when I returned to interview Chris for this book. The passage below captures how Chris's experiences with his own dad have helped shaped his vision to this day.

The Origins of a Dad's Vision Statement

CHRIS: My dad grew up in what was then a Polish neighborhood of Boston, Chelsea. His home life was very structured, and there were expected roles children were supposed to play. He told me a story once about Sundays in Chelsea — Sunday was visiting time. You go to church, and then you walk through the neighborhood, where all the relatives live, and do visits all afternoon. My dad, who was an only child, was expected to be seen and not heard. The adults had adult conversation, and he was usually not included in any of their activities. He determined that when he had children, he wasn't going to be like his dad. My wife's dad was the same way. So both men have made a really big effort to change with their own

children. I think that plays a large part in the way my wife and I are
raising our daughter.

When I was a kid, if my dad went to work on a Saturday or we
weren't in school, we had the option to go with him. We used to
love walking through the machine shop and seeing all the guys
working on lathes, and we loved walking through the blueprint
room. And then there was the diner. I remember when the guys
would change shifts and we'd hear them chatting; they'd be using
dirty language, and we just loved it. The guys talked to us and let
us hang out. We never heard anything like, "You kids don't belong
here."

Every vision is in some way rooted in history. In Chris's case, the
major source of inspiration for his Dad's Vision Statement, on the
next page, was clearly drawn from some positive aspects of his own
father's legacy. Interestingly, Chris's dad, like many men today, seems
to have been influenced by some of the more negative characteristics
of his parents.

Your Kids Are Not Just Accessories

CHRIS: The other day at the fire station, I watched Hayden play bas-
ketball with some of the guys. They lowered the hoop for her and
everything. I thought to myself, Isn't it great that they can include a
child like that? My wife and I have surrounded ourselves with people who are willing to do that. For the most part, if we go somewhere, we want to be able to bring our daughter and include her.
She's not an accessory that we take somewhere and plop down and
say, Okay, stay here, and when we're done, we'll get you. It's not
that way. We include Hayden in every area of our life.

I also think that playing with my daughter, in her world, helps to
build trust and keep our relationship strong. It can be too easy to
get caught up in paying bills and worrying about how much oil costs
and to lose our sense of imagination and playfulness. We can forget
how much fun it is to build a fort, do a puzzle, or splash in a pool.

EXERCISE 1. Dad's Vision Statement: CHRIS GARNIEWICZ

To create a Dad's Vision Statement, I asked Chris to imagine his daughter, Hayden, being interviewed for a documentary film about his life twenty years from now. Chris envisioned the filmmaker asking Hayden to describe her relationship with him. Then he responded to these four questions:

Twenty years from now, I hope Hayden says:
My dad is trustworthy and loving.
I can talk openly and honestly with him,
and he listens to my point of view.

Twenty years from now, I hope Hayden does not say:
Dad wasn't honest with me.
He didn't walk his talk.
He didn't care what I had to say.

Today, my priorities are:
I work hard at keeping my word and leading by my actions.
We include Hayden in every area of our lives
and spend tons of time with her.
We give her opportunities to try new things and to take risks,
encourage her to have a strong voice,
and help her make more decisions for herself.

What I need to change:
I need to come home from work in the morning and be less
grouchy, more patient, and more emotionally available.
I also need to be a better listener and to overall make a constant
effort to maintain trust and keep the dialogue open with Hayden.

When it rains — Hayden doesn't like thunderstorms — we build a little tent with cushions and sheets to hide under. Being human enough to still play opens you up so your child can see you as someone to relate to — not their best friend, but someone who understands them and their world. I think it fosters openness and builds trust.

We're also trying to raise our daughter to be independent and a good decision maker. What she chooses, she needs to run with, but we're not forcing her into anything. When it's something she has to do — like brushing her teeth or eating breakfast — we try to give her options and let her know the consequences of each, so she can decide for herself.

It can be as simple as letting her know she has to take a bath before bed. I would say, "You can do it before or after dinner. If you get it out of the way before dinner, you'll have more time after to read or play with your dolls. But if you do it later, that will cut into your playtime after dinner." And then the choice is hers. It's not necessarily an arguable option — she's still going to eat dinner and have a bath — but it's an option.

I think we've generated a really good open, trusting relationship. Hayden's not afraid to tell us what she likes or doesn't like. She has a voice. Hopefully, down the road this will lead to a much more open relationship with her as a teenager so that when issues arise, she'll feel that she can come to us with a problem, letting us know if she needs counseling, guidance, or a different perspective.

Being a Parent, Not a Friend

Chris and his wife, Larah, make it a priority to include their daughter in adult life — in the workplace, in social settings, in community activities. Their approach could not be much farther from what Chris's father experienced growing up — the "children should be seen and not heard" school of parenting. Not only is Hayden included in the adult world, but Chris makes a conscious effort to engage in her world of play and imagination as well. This mutual involvement is central to Chris's realizing his Dad's Vision Statement and to building a trusting, open relationship with Hayden. The difference in beliefs about parenting, in this case between generations, captures one of the central debates today about child-rearing: Are parents too permissive today, treating their children too much like friends or little adults?

Comedian Dana Carvey captured it perfectly in a hilarious HBO special *Squatting Monkeys Tell No Lies*. He first dramatizes a modern dad negotiating with his little boy: "Greggers, *what did we agree to?* Let's use our inside voices..." He quickly steps out of the modern dad character and follows with "Let's use our *inside voices*!!?...What ever happened to shut the f*ck up!": the other end of the spectrum.

My colleague Terry Real says, "Our relationship to our children is essentially like our other relationships to anyone else, with one striking difference: our children are clearly not our peers." He describes parenting as an example of a "healthy hierarchy." Being the one in charge, he says, is both easier and more difficult than our other relationships.[1]

It's easier, Real explains, because we don't look to our children to meet our dependency needs. We don't, for example, look to them to ease our worries about our finances or motivate us when we feel down. Consequently, they don't disappoint us in the way a spouse or a friend can by not meeting our needs. With our children we can truly love unconditionally. However, being in charge is more difficult because it requires that we show up and take responsibility for the fact that we are in the driver's seat. No matter how much noise and distraction is coming from the backseat, our children need us to keep our hands on the wheel. Often what's happening in the backseat is simply our children trying to find out if we are, in fact, actually in the driver's seat.

From a young age, children test to see exactly how well their parents set limits. The eternal question most of us ask is, "Am I being too easy or too strict?" Unfortunately, there is no easy answer to this question. I believe that it's our job to draw (and redraw) the line for what is acceptable and unacceptable behavior from our children. We must also communicate and follow through with realistic consequences when they step over that line. This helps establish that the choice — whether or not to step over that line — is very much up to them.

Chris gives his daughter a choice about how she manages her time in the evening. The key point he makes is that the choice is not whether she is going to take a bath, but *when* she will take a bath. When given these parameters, Hayden has to choose for herself how to manage her time. Chris and Larah demonstrate an inherent trust and assumption that she will make a decision that works best for her yet still keep to the bedtime rules. As long as her parents follow through if she doesn't take a bath, Hayden is likely to feel more empowered and trusted than if she was simply told what to do.

Another common way of disciplining a child is to use control — simply telling children what to do or what not to do. If they don't comply, they face consequences. While some situations require us to use control (to keep a child safe, to get her somewhere on time), overall this "father knows best" approach to discipline is ineffective and often backfires. In the long run, I believe, controlling a child teaches blind obedience and often leads to more rebellious behavior.

Some dads opt out of taking charge altogether and prefer, so to speak, to let their children sit in the front seat or even take a turn at the wheel. The "fun dad" doesn't like responsibility or rules. While this happens for many reasons — the dad has poor boundaries, lacks other adult male friendships, can't tolerate not being liked, leaves the limit-setting to his partner — I often find the underlying issues to be about guilt or fear. Many dads feel guilty about not being around enough, and/or they fear having the same distant relationship with their child that their own father may have had with them. So, naturally, being a friend or a "fun dad" can feel easier than being the "bad guy." Bad guys have to show up and set firm, consistent, and fair limits on a child. Not setting limits is a form of neglect and sets children up to think they are above the rules.

Chris's story is a great example of how important it is to integrate these different approaches to parenting. You don't have to be either an overindulgent "fun dad" or an authoritarian "bad guy." Children need both limits and love, discipline and fun. Chris understands that making time to build a fort on the living room floor is as much a part of developing the trust and connection he wants with his daughter as making sure she gets to bed on time.

Walking the Talk

CHRIS: As a firefighter, you're there to fix a problem. My job is to show up, do my best to help make things better, and then move on. But I can't come home and do that. I need to be able to come home and invest myself in the relationships with my wife and daughter; I've got to be willing to open up emotionally and deal with everything. We don't deal with emotions much at the fire department. We don't have to deal with Mr. Smith going into the hospital with burn injuries. I'm not saying we don't care, but it's just a switch you have to turn off.

When I get home from work, early in the morning, I need to restart my day so I can get rid of that portion of it and be an active member of the family. I get out of my uniform, take a shower, get a cup of coffee, read the paper for a few minutes. If I get out of work late, or if something keeps me from getting that full restart, I go into my own little shell or I get very grumpy. To have the patience to listen to Hayden can be very difficult. Fortunately, she likes to tell me when I'm being grumpy. Then I realize I need to take my time and decompress. I'm not necessarily a good listener. I really have to work at it.

Say, for example, Hayden's getting frustrated with a crafts project. Instead of telling her my opinion about how to solve the problem, I try to listen to her. I listen to why she's having trouble, ask her what she's trying to accomplish, and *then* maybe I pose some options and let her choose from those options. But I try not to give her the message that since I'm the adult I know best how to fix the situation.

Losing Focus on Your Vision

The most difficult part of living out your Dad's Vision Statement is first realizing and then actually making the changes you know must be made. Chris realizes that building an open, trusting relationship with Hayden requires that he learn to be a better listener. When he comes home from work still feeling the emotional weight of the night before or feeling cranky, the best and healthiest thing he can do is take time to decompress. Instead of using his job as an excuse for being such an impatient listener, Chris actively tries to do differently.

How well we listen often depends on situation and context. For example, when pulled over for speeding, I can suddenly become the most attentive listener you've ever seen. An hour later that attentiveness may disappear. I may find myself listening to my son Jake's story with one ear and listening to the baseball game on TV with the other. We need to remember that we all have the capacity to be great listeners. In fact, most dads use listening skills at work every day. Listening is a powerful form of caretaking and can greatly affect your child's sense of self-worth at any age. It's another way of saying "you are important." To be effective, however, you need to figure out what kind of listening is needed. The following steps outline essential skills as well as how and when to use them with children and adults. As you review these tips, think about which ones Chris exemplified with his daughter in the story above.

- *Confirm* what you hear by reflecting back to the speaker. When relevant, repeat what you heard the speaker say (use your words to describe what you hear). The key is to ask the speaker if you got it right, if you are on track. This is especially important to do with young children.

   "I hear you saying _____. Have I got that right?"

   "So, you did _____ and then you said _____. Does that capture it?"

- *Ask for clarification.* When you ask questions it shows that you're interested and following what the speaker is saying. Also, clarifying what happened or what a child is feeling gives you important information about the situation.

   "What did you do after that?"

   "What were you feeling at that point?"

- *Relate* personally to what your child is saying. Let the speaker know you understand what she is going through. This helps her know you're listening and not feel so alone. Even if you haven't had exactly the same experience, you can generalize. Be careful, however, not to turn the attention to yourself. Stay focused on the speaker.

   "I hear you. I've felt that way before, too."

   "That sounds similar to when…"

- *Offer your perspective, thoughts, impressions, suggestions.* Sometimes children won't ask, but they do want to hear what you have to say. It's best not to assume you know what they want. Instead, make an offer:

   "Is there anything you need or anything I can do?"

   "Would you like to hear what I think about what you said?"

MORE MODERN DADS: Antonio's Vision: Putting His Son First

Antonio Jiminez, 21
FAMILY: single dad with a son, two
BORN IN: Boston, Massachusetts
LIVES IN: Boston, Massachusetts
OCCUPATION: Massachusetts Bay Transit Authority
driver-in-training

The ease with which Antonio played with his busy toddler, Antonio Jr., while not missing a beat in our conversation, made me think this dad was a natural. I had the pleasure of spending a few afternoons and an evening with the two Antonios, interviewing Antonio's girlfriend, and meeting a few family members. Everyone agreed that Antonio is a committed dad who is working hard to walk his talk and create a vision for himself and his son. Realizing, for example, that he wanted to communicate better with his child's mother, Antonio enrolled in a relationship skills course. As you will see below, he is determined to be a better dad.

ANTONIO: Growing up, I didn't see many fathers. All my friends were being raised by mothers. I also saw kids being raised by the streets. Some tried to imitate their father, even though he wasn't there. Their father's in jail, so they feel like they have to follow in his footsteps, like, "My father wasn't no sucker, so I ain't going to be no sucker either."

Growing up without my father, with him locked up, I think the worst thing I could do is to get arrested. Because then my son would lose me forever, and that time with him is more precious than anything. So when I'm doing stuff, I've got to think, "Okay, what am I doing? Who else will it affect? It'll affect me, it'll affect my son and my whole family."

I want to be different. I feel there are things that my father could have told me about before I actually got into those situations, such as getting girls, having sex, or chilling with gang members. If my father had been there, he could have led me in different directions, and that's what I want to do for my boy so he won't have to go through what I've been through. And if he does see the stuff I've seen, I could tell him how to go about things differently instead of falling into the same traps.

Before my son was born, I was out in the streets, I was hanging with gang members. I used to beat up people. After having him, that's when I started thinking, "If I continue to hang out with these people, if I sell drugs, if I get arrested, who is this going to affect? It's going to affect him more than it's going to affect me." And I just didn't want him to have to go the same way.

So I decided that I didn't have to make myself seem tough by hanging out with those guys. For me to say no to chilling with them wasn't hard; I've got a son to think about, and some of those guys have nobody. I have friends who have been in and out of jail who just don't care anymore. I don't want that for myself.

I want Antonio Jr. going to a good school, getting a good education. I didn't get that much of an education. I learned pretty much everything from the streets and from watching other people. I just want my son to make all the right decisions that I didn't make. And I want him to see a better life, a better childhood. Because like I said, my father was gone by the time I was seven, so pretty much after seven I never had anybody to have that talk about the birds and the bees and all that. I just want him to have everything I didn't have in life.

There are so many stereotypes out there, about a young black man or a young Spanish guy: he's a thief, he's a gang member, he got his gun. As a father I want to tell my son to walk away, to keep moving, to use their stereotypes to make you better, so you can prove them wrong.

Your Dad's Vision Statement Is a Journey, Not a Destination

LARAH: I love to hear Chris and Hayden talking with each other when they're out working in the garage. It's not just that they're working on a project together; it's that they're side by side, on the same level, having conversations about others things too. That environment seems to open the channels to talk.

CHRIS: I really enjoy doing projects with Hayden. I'm Mr. Martha Stewart. I taught Hayden to sew. She hasn't fully gotten the hang of the sewing machine yet, but she has her own set of needles and threads and notions. Sometimes she helps me with an Art of Fire project — I do designs for helmets, uniform repairs, patches — or we may work on a little pillow for her doll, possibly a dress, or just go through the scrap bin for something to braid. I think that working together builds our relationship.

As a dad, and as a parent in general, I think that you've got to constantly make that effort to maintain the trust and the open dialogue. I think it's easy to get into a rut and shut down and say, Okay, my daughter trusts me, now I'm done. Trust and communication need to be reaffirmed. There's always more to do, but I think we have a really great relationship.

Who Will Be Your Witness?

The Dad's Vision Statement asks you to focus on yourself *in relationship*. Having another person, ideally someone close to you and your children, bear witness to your vision is crucial. By interviewing Larah and Chris together, as well as separately, I discovered that Chris's vision for his relationship with Hayden was not a surprise to Larah. Having a witness for your Dad's Vision Statement opens the door for support — whether that means getting help articulating a realistic vision, hearing feedback about the priorities you set, or talking through places you get stuck. Also, sharing your vision with someone else keeps you more accountable, though ultimately you are the only one who can make your vision a reality. Nevertheless, it can be very helpful just to get a reminder once in a while. You may decide to share your vision — and what it was like to create it — directly with your child (now or in the future), or perhaps with a friend, your partner, or another parent.

CHAPTER 2

Be the Bridge between Your Past and Your Future

In chapter 1, you started to develop a vision for the future. In his Dad's Vision Statement, Chris looked to his relationship with his own father as a model for parenting his daughter, Hayden. Whether or not you look to your father (or mother) as a model for parenting, the legacy of our parents, for better and for worse, lives inside each of us. Every modern dad — even those whose own parent(s) was absent — is faced with the challenge of exploring how that legacy has helped and hindered him, taking responsibility for the mistakes he's passed on to his kids, and finally, doing what's necessary to transform that legacy for future generations.

·In one of the opening lines of my documentary film, *All Men Are Sons: Exploring the Legacy of Fatherhood*, therapist and author Terry Real says, "Each man is a bridge spanning the generations that have come before him and the children that will come after him."[1] Our life, he explains, is literally the distance between those two points. In other words, as parents we always have one foot in the past and one in the future.

I use the bridge metaphor to emphasize a very important idea that many dads often forget or lose sight of: while certain aspects of a family legacy are beyond our control, the majority of what comes across the bridge from the past can at least be influenced, if not fully determined, by each of us. In my experience, most dads agree with this idea in their heads but don't necessarily believe it in their hearts.

When men describe the parts of their father's or family legacy they most fear repeating or passing on to their own children, I often hear a note of resignation in their voices. Usually they express their fear in the form of a joke about the inevitability of becoming — or already being — just like their father. For other men, this fear remains unspoken or unacknowledged. When I'm talking with a group of dads — or in a moment when I myself feel haunted by the past — a simple reminder can make a big difference in how we perceive the past at any moment: *legacy is not the same as destiny.*

Passing On What's Positive

Some men reflect on their parents' legacy and feel a deep sense of gratitude for the gifts they've been given, while others struggle to find anything to be thankful for at all. Exploring your past for a positive legacy is a spiritual opportunity to acknowledge not only your parents but also the generations that came before them. No matter what you discover, even if the one gift you are thankful for is the life you've been given, this process is also meant to reflect on two key questions: *How, specifically and concretely, will you pass on the gifts you've been given? What do you hope will be positive about your legacy?*

One dad I spoke with recently told me he wanted to pass on his parents' work ethic — his father was a plumber, his mother a part-time teacher and full-time homemaker. When I asked this dad how he was going to instill this work ethic in his children, he paused for a long time. It would be more difficult today, he explained, because his children were used to a much higher standard of living than he was as a child. In his working-class family, which never rose far above subsistence, nothing was taken for granted when he was a boy. It was always understood that the roof over their heads and the oil in the furnace were a direct result of his parents' hard work. Today, this dad explained, his children hardly understand *what* he does for work, much less how that work translates into things like clothes, heat, a roof over their heads, vacations, and so on. As he worked through this question, this dad concluded that it wasn't so much a work ethic he wanted to pass on to his children as it was an appreciation for the value of money and hard work.

As illustrated above, there is more to bridging the past and future than simply planning to keep all that was positive and change what was negative. Even dads with mostly positive legacies must do the work of actually figuring out how to pass them on and acting accordingly in an ever-changing world. I will certainly teach my kids to skate and ride a bike (not easy, by the way), but how will I pass on, in concrete, practical terms, my father's sense of humor and my mother's optimism?

Some believe that the search for something positive in their past is a waste of time or an indignity. Men who were abandoned (before birth or during childhood), abused, or neglected by their father, for example, are often resistant to examining the past.

I know firsthand how difficult, infuriating, and painful it can be to acknowledge "gifts" or anything positive from a father whose most apparent legacy was damage and disappointment. Paradoxically, so often the most treasured gifts from any father are discovered in the painful places that we are least likely to explore.

Transforming a negative legacy into something useful and positive is a difficult journey for most. Too often I meet dads who say their father is mostly a guide for what *not* to do as a parent; committing to "just do the opposite" may be enough to inspire some to make changes, but for many dads it's often a convenient way to avoid emotional pain from the past, a path that frequently leads to disillusionment. Making diamonds from coal, or in this case seeing a wonderful gift in what used to be just a bad memory, is a *process*.

Whether we've been given a lot to be thankful for or struggle to find much at all, each of us will be responsible for the gifts we do and do not pass on to the next generation. Looking back and acknowledging our ancestry is also a reminder that we — as well as our children — are part of something greater than ourselves, bigger than this particular moment in history.

Some dads who spent their childhood without a father in the picture discover a need or desire to revisit their past for the sake of their own children. In his mid-forties, for example, Bobby Lee Smith (whom we'll learn much more about in chapter 4) realized that if he wanted his teenage daughter to truly know herself, he had an obligation to connect her with his family history. With a father who left when he was four — and whom he only met twice afterward — Bobby had the courage and determination to go on a difficult emotional journey for the sake of his daughter. While far from a storybook ending, he did succeed in reconnecting with a father he hadn't seen in over three decades as well as in introducing his daughter to a larger extended family he hadn't even known existed.

The gift Bobby gave his daughter and future generations, however, was not about the outcome of finding his father — his search, as many do, could have ended very differently. The act of facing his personal demons — anger, resentment, indifference, fear, hurt — in an effort to transform a legacy of disconnection into something positive was, in itself, the true gift he gave.

Past Problems, Future Liabilities

We cannot protect our children from the mistakes of our father if we are not courageous enough to explore how his legacy affected us as boys, as men, and as dads today. Problems from the past, if ignored, usually become problems in the future. For many men, the legacy of a father can be loaded with powerful feelings of anger, disappointment, sadness, and/or grief. If we do not deal with these feelings, we will likely pass them on to our children. Addictions and trauma expert Pia Mellody describes this psychological process as "carried feelings."[2] This concept is crucial to understanding the very real implications for children if we ignore, deny, or lose touch completely with painful emotions we may still harbor from the past.

I could not hope to protect my children from the legacy of rage my father left me if I refused to face many painful feelings and difficult truths. Being on the receiving end of my father's anger — which I believe was born from his own father repeatedly calling him "stupid" and "no good" — left me feeling as if I was fundamentally a bad person. The difficult truth I've had to contend with, as silly and parody worthy as that sounds, is simply that I am not, in fact, a bad person.

To protect my children from that legacy means that instead of running away from the pain and anger inside me, I try to deal with it in healthy ways, such as finding different outlets for my grief and learning about true self-worth. Imagine, conversely, if I did the opposite and used alcohol to dull or escape my pain; my young children would undoubtedly feel abandoned, resentful, confused, angry, and responsible for my behavior (when a parent falls apart or explodes, the child usually blames himself). They would feel exactly what I was busy escaping: pain. In other words, they would *carry* my pain for me. The choice of how to deal with that pain would eventually, as they grew up, become theirs to make. This legacy would continue generation after generation until one person in the family finally decided to stop the pain and begin the work of healing and transformation.

Think of the negative parts of the legacy from your own parents as liabilities to manage for the sake of your children and future generations. *Liability* is defined as "the likelihood or probability of something happening; as anything for which somebody is responsible, especially a debt; and as something that holds somebody back." As the saying goes, "Pass it back, or pass it on."[3]

Every parent leaves a legacy. Awareness of the role we play in bridging the past and future means little without action; both are useless without consistency. Just as lifting weights every month or two won't build muscle, an occasional change in behavior or flash of insight is unlikely to make much difference in the legacy you leave. Legacies can be elusive — what is alcoholism in one generation may become workaholism in the next — and generational change hard to come by. As my friend Bill says, "practice makes permanent."

The following story brings to life one man's ongoing journey to bridge the past and future. When he sat down to write a series of letters to his father (an exercise later in the chapter), Juan had no idea that putting pen to paper would unleash a flood of memories, questions, and realizations. His story illustrates how family legacies play out in different ways over time, and why the past is always relevant to the present moment.

Juan Lozada, 39

FAMILY: married; father of two daughters, three and five
BORN IN: Bolivia, Colombia
LIVES IN: Somerville, Massachusetts
OCCUPATION: owner of a business technology company,
     PFT, Inc.

I met Juan at a talk I gave for the Somerville Family Network, a great community organization in Boston with an active fathers' group. As usual, a bunch of dads stuck around to ask questions. After a few moments, I noticed that there were now four of us, including Juan, all standing in a circle, chatting away. I had been looking for a group of dads nearby to pilot some of the exercises for this book. Before I said anything, Juan suggested we get together at his house as a group. Amazingly, only weeks later, I found myself in Juan and his wife, Sharon's, living room with the same group of four dads.

Juan's story floored me. As he described life growing up on a farm in Colombia with twelve siblings, a father who was blind, and a mother who quietly kept everything running, I was captivated by the telling as much as by the story itself. When he returned to our next meeting with nearly a notebook full of his responses to the legacy exercises, it was clear to me that Juan wasn't just answering questions; he was on a journey.

In the first interview I did with Juan, he said that by writing he had started to "connect the dots" — to reconcile the tough father he knew as a boy with the aging father he reconnected with as an adult, and finally with the now-deceased father whose legacy lives on inside him.

A Legacy of Survival

JUAN: My life at first was pretty simple. I finished school and went to college. I graduated, found a career, and started working. I had it all — up to that point. My job, working for a veterinarian, had me driving from farm to farm outside Bolivia. One morning, on a country road at about 7:00, I was stopped by a group of guys — all very young and heavily armed — from the rebel group FARC. In Colombia they kidnap people for ransom money or because they need someone with certain skills, like a doctor or veterinarian, or just because they want you to join. There I was, twenty-two years old, and suddenly my whole life was turned upside down. I was told to get out of my car and had no choice but to go with them.

We walked until we reached a riverbed — which I knew was not good, because with riverbeds you leave no tracks or traces — and this guy pointed his gun at me and said, "Just keep walking and don't look back." I felt this coldness in my back as I started up the riverbed, then I fell to my knees and burst into tears. Man, please don't kill me. I just lay there flat, and nothing happened. The guy just grabbed my arm, and we all kept walking. I don't know what happened in that moment. I think God gave me a second chance.

During the next two weeks, I talked to one rebel — he was a kid, maybe fifteen — and tried to understand where he was coming from. He had no education, he had been abused by his father, he lived in a violent home with no food. So now he has a gun and he feels powerful. I told him about my father — who wasn't abusive like his but was not easy to connect with — and tried to get him to see that his past didn't have to control his future. I was trying to pull out any little drop of love he had. There must have been a little left because one night, after talking, this kid let me go. He said, "You walk out of here tonight with no guarantees," meaning that if they caught me, they would probably kill me. I had to take the chance. It took me about three or four days of walking to get back to civilization. That was the beginning of my journey.

After a year of being persecuted for escaping — they know where you work, where you're from, who your family members are — I had to leave Colombia. For the next six months, country after country, from Panama up through to Mexico, I made my way to the United States. *That* was the journey of my life. After twelve years, I finally got my citizenship last year.

My father taught me never to give up, to take what each day brings. He was the hardest-working man I've ever met. He started working on a farm at age thirteen and never stopped. For the last thirty years of his life he was blind but didn't complain once. He just kept going.

Life is full of the unexpected. Sometimes you have things, and then they disappear. You have to start from scratch. My father did, and so did I. He gave me these gifts, that I want to pass to my kids — the capacity to stand strong, to keep striving, to never give up. I don't take anything for granted. Today I can provide my daughters with a better life, and I savor every minute with them.

In Juan's harrowing story we're reminded of how sometimes we don't even realize we've been given a gift until later — sometimes many years later. Juan had always admired his father's strength and resolve, but it wasn't until this traumatic incident and his subsequent journey to America that Juan truly appreciated this tremendous gift from his father's legacy. To give a far less dramatic example, it wasn't until I was scrambling to lace up my four-year-old's skates recently that I realized, and fully appreciated, my dad's patience and commitment to teaching me to ice skate.

In the exercise on the following page, Identify the Gifts and Liabilities from Your Father, I asked Juan to review the two lists and circle a few of the gifts his father gave him, as well as a few of the liabilities from his legacy. Take a moment to look over the list (abridged here) and the items Juan circled, then continue reading.

A Legacy of Absence and Anger

JUAN: My father was the man of the house. He supported the family, he put food on the table, but he had very little to do with the kids (and there were twelve of us). He didn't change diapers, he didn't clean or cook or anything like that. In his generation, that was the woman's job. He was always working very hard on our farm, though he was

EXERCISE 2. Identify the Gifts and Liabilities from Your Father: JUAN LOZADA

Below is a partial list of gifts your father may have given you and liabilities he may have left you with. I asked Juan to circle as many as
apply to his relationship with his father.

GIFTS	LIABILITIES
A good work ethic	didn't control anger
honest	sexist attitude
warm/caring/loving	overly critical
empathetic	unwilling to ask for help
good listener	often or completely absent
handled conflict responsibly	not a good teacher
strong willed	wouldn't talk about his feelings
sense of humor	uninvolved in parenting
stands up against injustice	

completely blind. He could do a lot of stuff, but at the same time he
couldn't do many other things, like play, run around, jump, and throw.
My mom had to play both roles, not just with parenting with but running the farm, doing the finances, and looking out for our education.
This led to a lot of frustration and struggle that brought out the
other side of my father: his temper. He could be very explosive and
aggressive. As a child, I was mostly afraid of him.

I never really connected with my father until he was older. I
decided that if he wasn't going to approach me, then I would reach
out to him. I started putting little pieces together. One day I realized
that I'd never gotten a hug from him. So I thought to myself, what

if I tried to hug him? What would happen? I gave it a try, and he hugged me back. Wow! The toughest guy I know just hugged me back. Why hadn't I ever seen this person? Maybe he didn't want to show who he was when he was younger. I suddenly saw a light in him I didn't know was even there. I saw a different person.

I got to know my dad better than I ever had in that last year of his life. He died about a year after we started this new relationship. I realized a lot of things. I felt sympathy for him because of his illness, the lack of love he had growing up, and the pain he suffered. I was angry with him at the same time, for not taking responsibility for some of the things he did, but also for not opening up this door earlier. That was about seven years ago.

He was an amazing person, but he went through tough times. What I want to change with my kids is the angry explosions. I want them to feel loved and connected to me, not afraid.

One gift Juan got from his father was toughness, his ability to persevere under the most difficult of circumstances. However, this toughness, often expressed through explosive anger and rage by his father, has also become a liability to Juan. *The challenge in looking back at a legacy for so many men is how to hold what appear to be contradictory images of one person.* What makes this possible for Juan, and for any man, is his willingness to empathize. By developing a deeper emotional understanding of his father's life — by seeing him as the boy who grew up in harsh conditions, the man whose blindness burdened and strengthened him, the father who put food on the table, as well as the old man who longed to give his son a hug — Juan has cultivated his own capacity for managing the complexity of his father's legacy. While he does have great empathy for his father, Juan is also very clear about the mistakes his father made.

In the follow-up exercise below, Bridge the Past and Future, Juan is asked to think more concretely and practically about how he will protect his children from the liabilities, and how he will pass on the gifts, from his father.

EXERCISE 3. **Bridge the Past and Future:** JUAN LOZADA

I asked Juan to choose two of the gifts he'd circled and two of the liabilities from the preceding activity, on page 44, and to fill in the charts below.

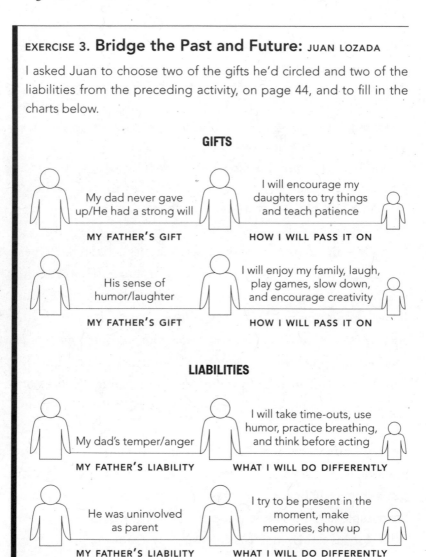

GIFTS

My dad never gave up/He had a strong will

MY FATHER'S GIFT

I will encourage my daughters to try things and teach patience

HOW I WILL PASS IT ON

His sense of humor/laughter

MY FATHER'S GIFT

I will enjoy my family, laugh, play games, slow down, and encourage creativity

HOW I WILL PASS IT ON

LIABILITIES

My dad's temper/anger

MY FATHER'S LIABILITY

I will take time-outs, use humor, practice breathing, and think before acting

WHAT I WILL DO DIFFERENTLY

He was uninvolved as parent

MY FATHER'S LIABILITY

I try to be present in the moment, make memories, show up

WHAT I WILL DO DIFFERENTLY

Not Heroes, Not Villains

At different points in our lives we pause and look back. Sometimes what triggers this is a milestone event: the passing of a parent, the birth of a child, a wedding, a divorce, an illness. Other times something less dramatic prompts reflection: a phone call from a sibling, the look on a child's face, a familiar place. Or it may be a gut feeling, an inexplicable urge, or, as in Juan's case, a sudden awareness of time passing.

In his early thirties, living a new life far from Colombia, Juan reached out to his aging father. To his surprise, the tough, hot-tempered farmer had transformed into a sweet, if sad, old man. Besides getting to experience the loving side of his father, if only for one short year, Juan also opened up a potentially confusing new reality: his father, like all people, was complex in ways he would never fully understand. Sometimes the one-dimensional, black-and-white version of a father — the "angry father" or the "loving father" — is easier to make sense of than the three-dimensional father who appears both angry and loving or both distant and connected. Juan's response was to move toward the contradictions, to look at his father's shades of gray so as to better understand the legacy that had been passed on to him.

It is imperative that we come to view our fathers (even if absent) realistically, not in black-and-white terms. If we idealize our dads, we may miss the liabilities we carry. This would be like Juan holding only the image of his father as a survivor who taught his children to be tough but denying the more damaging dimensions of his dad, such as his explosive anger. In this case, Juan would be more likely to pass on the pain he once felt — as the boy on the other end of his father's fury — to his own children.

If, on the other hand, we can only degrade our father, refusing to see anything positive, we may blind ourselves to important lessons he may have taught or remain unaware of potential qualities he may have instilled. We may instead cling to resentment as a badge or as justification for our own bad behavior. In Juan's case, if he had held on only to the image of his father as disconnected, bitter, and rageful, never seeing himself as a survivor — like his father — perhaps he wouldn't have made it through his kidnapping ordeal.

By seeing our fathers as flawed human beings who did their best with what they had, we remain humble as fathers ourselves, knowing that someday we'll be in their shoes. With this understanding, we can more clearly see the mistakes we've made, own up to them, and do better today and tomorrow. Our children will also be able to see us not as heroes or as villains, but as flawed men, trying to be the best dads we can. Juan, for example, recognizes that he needs to keep learning how to manage his anger.

Doing Anger Differently

JUAN: If you didn't do something my father wanted, he would explode: "If you don't do it, *I'll* do it for you!" He would drag you to where he wanted you to go. At other times the explosion came when he felt pushed into a corner. I can recognize that the angry part of my father is still in me, and I work very hard to avoid that with my kids. I want them to feel loved and connected, not afraid of their dad.

One of the challenges for me is how fast the anger comes. I try to recognize that moment so I can react differently. It happens sometimes in the morning when I'm getting my daughter ready for school. I say, "Time to brush your teeth." "No, I don't want to brush my teeth, I'm playing with my dolls." Then I start getting into the mode of, "Yes, you're going to brush them because *we've* got to go." "No, I don't want to . . ." and then I get upset and just pick her up and pretty much put her at the sink. "Here," I say, taking her hand, "is how you brush your teeth." It just escalates from there. Instead, I'm trying to just remove myself from the situation and take a few minutes to calm down or figure something else out. Breathing really helps too.

I think what frustrates kids the most is when they're doing something and we ask them to do something else right away. So the approach I've taken lately is to provide a transition from what they're doing. Let's say she's playing with a doll. I might say, "Okay, why don't we bring your doll into the bathroom." Once in the bathroom, I say, "Do you want to brush your teeth with your doll?" And then she brushes her teeth. I try to build in more time. Some days, it's going to take me maybe another extra ten minutes. Why not relax about this, make a joke, and play with it, and still try to move it along? Otherwise we get into the same struggle.

Healthy and Unhealthy Anger

Expressing anger in a relationship with a child — or in any relationship, for that matter — is not always unhealthy. The critical question is *how* you express that anger: responsibly and nonviolently or abusively (either verbally or physically)? When, for example, Juan described stepping out of the room to breathe, he was being responsible with his anger. Another great move he made was trying to shift the energy by engaging with his daughter in her world of dolls; though it feels like the last thing you want to do in the moment, making even just a subtle shift in energy — away from the heaviness of a power struggle and toward the lightness of play or even humor — can make an immediate difference.

The fact is, anger is a legitimate and important emotion that everybody, kids included, experiences. It's not about making it go away; rather, it's about managing it in a healthy, nondestructive way. Below are some suggestions for dads, like Juan, who struggle with anger.

Responsible expressions of anger include

- Taking full ownership of your feelings by using an "I" statement ("I am so angry").

- Resisting the urge to direct your anger at someone else or to blame them for how you feel. Remove the phrase "you make me" from your vocabulary, because it implies that you are a victim, that you simply have no control over your feelings. Instead use the phrase, "When you do ___, I feel ___." Example: "When you don't come after I've called three times, I get very, very angry."

Now imagine that Juan had reacted more like his father when his daughter refused to brush her teeth and shouted, "Get in here now, or…" and slammed the medicine cabinet door shut. This kind of direct verbal threat, as well as an implied threat (slamming the door), crosses the line from responsible to abusive anger.

Verbally and/or physically abusive expressions of anger* include

- Control, retaliation, or punishing withdrawal
- Explicit or nonverbal threats, such as slamming doors, pounding a table, throwing things, or getting in someone's face
- Hitting, grabbing, or pushing someone
- Yelling, screaming, or name calling
- Shaming (using ridicule and sarcasm) or humiliating someone
- Telling someone (child or adult) what he/she should do, think, or feel

Verbally and physically abusive expressions of anger directed at children or acted out in their presence damage their self-worth and

---

* Abusive behavior is not always the result of misdirected anger. Often it is due to the abusive person's desire to use coercive control against their intimate partners, children, and others. In such cases, it is essential that the abusive person seek professional help, preferably from a certified batterer's intervention program. To find a certified program, call your local domestic violence hotline.

teach them to repeat the same behaviors as they grow up. Recent studies have found that witnessing abuse in the home can negatively affect children just as much as if they had been abused themselves.[4]

Chances are you've demonstrated one or more of these behaviors at some point, in varying degrees. It's important to realize that you don't need to engage in any of these behaviors anymore. I sometimes hear men get defensive and say things like, "I lose my temper, but not very often." It is *never* okay to "lose it" and become verbally abusive with a child or partner. No matter how infrequent, these behaviors must be stopped.

Some dads who grew up in homes where verbally and/or physically abusive expressions of anger were the norm may use such justifications to avoid facing the reality of how damaged they were by those behaviors. In contrast, facing that reality could potentially unleash years of pain and threaten to destroy the idealized version of their father they may have kept intact since boyhood.

Like most children, I blamed myself for my father's rage. He remained idealized, blameless, and unaccountable throughout my childhood. It wasn't until I developed a drinking problem as a teenager that — with the help of a therapist — I started to realize the reality of who he was and how I was following in his footsteps.

As Juan explores his mother's legacy in the next section, you will see in detail how a father's anger can directly affect his child, as well as his child's relationship with his mother. Juan describes how, when dealing with conflict now, as an adult, he realizes how the most unhealthy aspects of both his father's and mother's legacies have been passed on to him. Amazingly, he embodies both sides of the conflict he grew up witnessing, behaving at times with his father's rage and at other times with his mother's silence. You will also see how Juan then does the work of healing and forgiveness in order to transform this legacy.

A Mother's Legacy

As dads, the obvious connection many of us make when we think about legacies from the past is to our own fathers. Even those of us who grew up in female-headed homes with no male present — in my case, my incredible mother raised my brother and me on her own from ages two to eight — still tend to look to the image of the father as the central influence on how we parent.

As I mentioned earlier, some men truly see their father's absence as a gift and successfully "do the opposite"; however, many will say that their father's absence is a gift, when in reality they still harbor enormous resentment and pain. The key difference, generally speaking, is whether or not that man has done the emotional work of grieving (more on this topic later in the chapter).

No matter what kind of dad we had — completely absent, part-time, fly-by, or fully present — and how huge an influence our dad had on us, our mother's legacy is also very much inside each of us. At the mere mention of mother-son relationships, typically what first comes to mind (and what one first comes across in a Google search) is not a mom's influence on the kind of father her boy may become. More likely you'll find words like *Oedipus, clingy, dysfunction, marriage problems*, and *feminization*. In a culture that simultaneously reveres mothers and degrades them (especially single mothers, for the absurd notion that they are "feminizing boys") we lose sight of the enormous influence — negative and positive — that mothers have on how we as adult sons parent our children. Words such as *strength, commitment, sacrifice*, and *courage* are just as attributable to mothers as *care, emotions*, and *nurture*.

My own mother was fed all sorts of myths and lies about the consequences of raising a son without a dad. In short, they warned her I would become gay and effeminate. Thankfully, she decided that raising me with a raging alcoholic father — who was a very ill man at the time — would do far more damage. The irony of this situation, and why looking at a mother's legacy is so important, is that some of those so-called "feminine" qualities my mother was warned about are today the very qualities I treasure and find essential to my fathering — nurturing, listening, and silliness. And, echoing my best friend, who happens to be a single dad, my mother also "taught me to be tough, to stick through things that are hard."

Just like dads, mothers also make mistakes that get handed down through the generations. However, I have found that men are often reticent to explore their mother's negative legacy. Perhaps it's because as boys so many relied on mom as the primary caregiver and learned not to bite the hand that feeds. Or, as in my situation, sometimes the father's mistakes are much more blatant than the mother's. It wasn't until many years after I had begun exploring my father's legacy that I finally realized I also carried both gifts and liabilities from my mother. Juan, too, now sees clearly the impact of his mother's legacy.

On the following page are excerpts of Juan's responses to a longer series of questions about the gifts and liabilities of his mother's legacy.

A Legacy of Silence and Strength

JUAN: My mother gave us the gift of education. My father was reluctant to do so because he wanted us to be part of the farm, but eventually he gave in and contributed to helping us become educated. She's still alive, and I support her as much as I can because she gave me the opportunity, she opened the door. Her idea was if you learn, you can have a better life.

For much of her life, she suffered quietly under my father. He used his anger to get his way. He was the all-powerful. My mom never had a voice in the relationship; she didn't make the decisions.

EXERCISE 4. Explore Your Mother's Legacy: JUAN LOZADA

1. **What gifts did your mother give you that you intend to pass on to your children?**
   My mother gave me the gift of education, a positive attitude, and strength

2. **What liabilities has she left you that you don't want to give to your children?**
   She didn't talk about who she was or what she wanted. I don't want to hide from problems. I don't want to pass this on to my girls.

3. **Were there ways she interacted with your father that were healthy and positive?**
   She insisted on education and made sure my dad knew it was important.

4. **Were there ways she interacted with your father that were unhealthy or upsetting to you?**
   She suffered quietly and didn't stand up to him and his abusive behavior.

So I picked up mixed messages about relationships. If someone is upset with me for a mistake I actually didn't make, I may just swallow it and be passive. In a different situation, I may react the opposite, more like my father. I think the difference is that if I don't know the person, I tend to be more like my mother. If it's someone I know and trust, I'm more like my dad, just not as explosive. Finding the middle ground is my challenge.

If my father would have allowed my mom just to be herself, I think that she would be much happier. And if she could have stood up for herself, she would be a different person today. Now that I have two girls, I want them to believe that they have power, they have a voice. My wife is my best friend, and I love for her to be herself. I am not a shadow cast over her like my father was with my mother. My wife is showing my girls that Mom can do things, that Mom is powerful, that Mom makes decisions.

Together, we show them two people who love and respect each other. We communicate, we work things out. We share responsibilities around the house. Cooking and cleaning aren't a woman's job, they're everybody's job. In Colombia, my brothers-in-law look at me when I'm in the kitchen, like, What are you doing in there? I tell them that their attitude is just an excuse to be lazy.

MORE MODERN DADS: **A Grandfather's Legacy**

James Threalkill, 43

FAMILY: divorced; father of three daughters, fifteen, four, and two
BORN IN: Denver, Colorado
LIVES IN: Nashville, Tennessee
OCCUPATION: national diversity director, Skanska International; nationally renowned visual artist

---

I met James when he was teaching at Montgomery Bell Academy, a boy's school in Nashville. Years later, he and his daughter participated in a dad-daughter communication workshop I was leading at his daughter's school. Knowing very few details about James's fatherhood story, I knew in my gut that James would end up in this book. After spending some time with him, I've discovered James to be a study in contrasts and the embodiment of what it means to be a whole person.

James is strong and bighearted. His undeniable physical presence is tempered by a sense of ease and gentleness. James has a booming voice but seems to be more interested in listening. More than being just a good listener, James is contemplative.

James is also a nationally recognized visual artist. Given

his stature and athletic gait, discovering that James played football under Bill Parcells at Vanderbilt University was less than shocking. This artist-teacher-athlete is also currently a business executive at a transnational construction company, Skanska International.

Most important, James is a deeply committed dad and mentor who cherishes the legacy handed down to him by his grandfather and father (and mother), best described as a legacy of self-respect, decency, dignity, hard work, and care. James is intent on passing on these gifts to the next generation — his own children, as well as a wider community of boys and men.

Boys Need Men

JAMES: I was the oldest of six kids growing up, four boys and two girls. We respected our father. And we saw how our grandfather, our mother's father, was also a very strict disciplinarian in terms of how we were taught to treat people and the way we conducted ourselves. Back when I was growing up, on those Saturday mornings when you thought that you were going to be sleeping in and watching cartoons, my grandfather would come and knock on the door at seven and get me and my brother, my second-oldest brother, up to go out to Nashville's most affluent neighborhoods to do yard work. He would take us with him to mow the lawns and do the landscaping. And though my grandfather didn't have a lot of education, some of Nashville's wealthiest citizens still maintained a level of respect for him because he didn't tolerate being treated otherwise.

He also constantly told us, "If you stay in school and work hard you won't have to be doing this. You'll own one of these houses instead of being out here working in the yard. But there's nothing wrong with hard work." So having a strong work ethic, maintaining a level of self-respect and dignity, and having immense love for his daughter and doing anything and everything that he could for her were things that I learned from my grandfather about what a father is. I saw him as a really strong man.

I had strong figures like my father and my grandfather, but a lot of boys and young men only have to look to the entertainment and sports industry to learn how they should conduct themselves, aside from the people who are on the street. When I was growing up, a thug was something your parents told you you didn't want to be. And now it is considered cool. Guys are tattooing their chests with the message "I'm a thug." I think this has a lot to do with the absence of fathers that we're seeing today. Then, add to this a marketing culture that uses sexuality to promote and sell just about any product. More boys are becoming sexually active a lot earlier than they were in the past. And these boys or young men are *not* in a position to be fathers, because they don't have the wherewithal to take care of themselves, let alone other children.

There are currently over a million black men in prison. There's a really prevalent subculture of dysfunction, and if more men don't take responsibility for this situation, it's going to get even worse. I know guys who I went to high school with that are coming together to form men's groups and who can serve as mentors for young men. These are some of the ways that men can be available and take responsibility for boys and young men who are fatherless. But it's a tremendous challenge. I've got my own children, but I still try to work with some young men who could benefit, because I want to have an impact on the community.

Having a Heart-to-Heart with Your Dad . . . Whether or Not He Is Present

Juan describes how his mother did not have a voice in her relationship with his father. Likewise, much was left unspoken between
Juan and his father. Juan and his mother were both afraid to speak
truthfully of their experience — how frightening it was to live under
his tyranny, how hurtful he was, or how much they needed him to
be different. Even as an adult, when his dad was no longer physically
threatening, Juan remained fearful of speaking truthfully to him.

Like so many modern dads — including those who grew up
with healthier, nonabusive fathers — Juan wants his own kids to do
the exact thing he struggled to do with his father: to be trusting and
truthful, even when it's hard. The last thing Juan, or almost any dad,
would want is to find out years from now that his children were
afraid of him, or avoided talking about matters of the heart, or
didn't think he was interested in what they had to say. Yet, as adult
sons, like Juan, many of us withhold such revelations from our own
fathers until illness or old age sets in. Even then, speaking about love
and pain can feel less like a hill and more like a mountain. All too frequently, as was the case with Juan, sons wait until it's too late.

As you will see in the following sections, however, Juan discovered that it is still possible to have a heart-to-heart talk with your father, even if he has passed on, is no longer in your life, or not in an
active, ongoing relationship with you.

Why Bother Saying What's Never Been Said?

Having an open, honest talk with your father is valuable for three
reasons:

1. It allows you to acknowledge your gratitude for the im-
    portant role he's played in your life.

2. It gives you the opportunity to hold him accountable for the mistakes he's made and to move toward forgiveness.

3. It paves the way for developing an open, honest dialogue and deeper connection with your children.

Letting your father know how thankful you are is among the greatest gifts you as a son can give. What father would not want to hear about the positive legacy he's passed on to his children? Whether you thank him for the sacrifices he's made, the values he's instilled, or simply the life he's given you, each man has this gift to give his father.

Holding your father accountable for his mistakes is also a gift you can give. As I mentioned in the introduction, when I described to my father the ways his anger damaged me as a boy and how I still struggled with this legacy as a man, he didn't know what to say. Yet, three crucial things happened as a result of that exchange. First, he eventually apologized for hurting our family — something he may not have done if I hadn't held him accountable. Second, I gained self-respect by having had the courage to be honest with him. Finally, when he died years later, it was a peaceful death; he no longer carried guilt for his mistakes. He left knowing that nothing was left unspoken between us and that he had been forgiven.

There is a difference between holding someone accountable and blaming him. For example, the responsibility for how I handle my father's legacy belongs to me, no matter how great his mistakes were. I alone must fill the empty spaces and cool the rage left by my father. Holding him accountable, letting him know the damage he did, paved a way to forgiveness; blame would have made forgiveness impossible. And forgiveness is an essential step toward creating a hopeful legacy for your children.

How to Have the Talk

The following exercise, which involves writing three different letters to your dad, is a way to have the "talk" with your father, as Juan did, between your own two ears. You may decide to send or read these letters to your father; you may not. You may decide to read them to a friend or partner. This exercise is more about the process of writing the letters and getting out what's inside you. What you do with them once they're written is up to you.

If you find yourself resisting this activity or having difficulty writing anything negative about your father, this may be owing to one of the following reasons:

- You feel disloyal, selfish, or mean writing about your father's negative behaviors. Remember, every parent makes mistakes, including you. It is the job of each generation to look back, acknowledge these mistakes, show gratitude for the gifts, and try to do better with their own children. Acknowledging the mistakes does not mean you are saying that your father didn't try his best, or that he wasn't a good dad, or that you don't love him. You can celebrate the positive and be honest about the negative at the same time.

- You feel like you're complaining or being self-pitying. There is a big difference between self-pity and self-empathy. Imagine this scenario: First, try to recall your father's negative behaviors when you were young. Maybe he was overly critical or didn't show up to important events. Now, imagine demonstrating those same behaviors to your children. How would they feel if you didn't show up or you constantly criticized them? Terrible, right? So try to show the same empathy you have with your own children for the "little boy" part of yourself. Just as they would feel terrible, you probably did (as a boy) too.

EXERCISE 5. **Write Three Letters to Your Father . . . Whether or Not He Is Present***

 Letter One: Write to your father about what it was like for you to grow up with (or without) him. Describe what was positive as well as what was difficult or negative. Think about the things you've wanted to say to him but never have. You may cover your entire childhood or choose to focus on a particular time period or specific incident.

 Letter Two: Write *from your father's perspective* (the letter should start "Dear Son."). This letter should capture what you imagine your father would say to you in response to letter one. How would your father react to that letter? Would he accept your point of view? Would he argue with certain things? Would he be loving, hurt, or angry?

 Letter Three: Write again *from your father's perspective*. This letter should capture what you wish your father's response would be. In other words, if he were to respond in the best possible way to reading letter one, what would he say? This letter is a way for you to imagine your father giving you everything you wished he had.

Following is an excerpt from a letter that Juan wrote to his father seven years after his father had died. In it he expresses his gratitude but also lets his father know what a huge impact his anger had on the family. The letter demonstrates how Juan is able to manage

---

*   This exercise was adapted from the work of Belinda Berman, LCSW.

powerfully conflicting feelings about his father: anger and gratitude, love and pain. He does not overidealize his father's positive legacy and is careful to resist the temptation to vilify or denigrate him for what is also a very painful legacy. Instead, Juan has the courage to see his father realistically, as just another imperfect human being not so unlike himself.

EXERCISE 5. Letter One: JUAN LOZADA

I asked Juan to write to his father about what it was like for you to grow up with him. I asked Juan to describe what was positive as well as what was difficult or negative.

Dear Dad:

I want to thank you for giving me life. I had some great moments with you, but not until almost at the end of your life; I wish I had spent more time with you, and I wish you could have seen me as a father. You gave us life, fed us, dressed us, kept a roof over our heads, yet there were things I wished I could have received from you, such as better communication, more play when I was a child, and the chance to spend time just being with you. It was particularly hard to be around you when you lost your temper and exploded. That has impacted my life tremendously. I will never forget when I looked at my mom and could see tears coming down her face, since you were yelling and screaming. She was always affected by your behavior and still is to this day. As I look back and dig deeper to find answers, I think how hard it must have been for you not having a father figure. You had no support, no chance to play and have fun, and you had to work so hard as a boy. . . .

Juan's Reflections on Writing the Letter

JUAN: When I was writing these letters, especially the ones from my father's perspective, it almost felt like I was talking with him. It opened up communication between us on a spiritual level, even though he's not around. I got to tell him what's on my mind, the honest things I feel about him but have never said. So, in a way, by writing I am left with two visions of my father: one is thankful that he gave what he could, despite his very difficult life, and the second is angry that he never took responsibility for the pain he caused. Whatever was behind his anger, we were the ones who bore the brunt of it. He never apologized for that. By writing, I had the chance to say, "You were an asshole for this, and you were really great in this other way."

If I had written this while my father was alive, I think I would be calling him and talking with him right now. It makes me sad that I didn't do this while he was alive. I should have stayed with him more. I should have hugged him twenty years ago instead of waiting until his last year. Why didn't I come up to my father and say, "Let's go play"? Was it because he was blind or so "tough"? Why did I wait so long? I guess I didn't realize it until now. . . .

I want to change this history by accepting *all* of who my father was, who I am right now, and what I can still give my daughters. The play, the fun, the sense of connection I didn't have with him, I am now creating with my own children.

The wisdom Juan gained by doing the seemingly simple exercises in this chapter is profound. While he regrets not exploring his relationship with his father earlier in his life, Juan was able to develop a new and different kind of connection, even in his father's absence. His willingness to journey back through the rugged emotional landscape of his childhood on the family farm in Colombia was an essential first step in coming to terms with the father he both loved and loathed.

By giving voice to the parts of himself that were hurt and damaged by his father's violence, as well as the parts that were strengthened by his enduring love, Juan freed himself from bitter-ness and opened himself up to forgiveness. By reflecting, by taking risks such as reaching out to his dad later in life, by writing letters and talking with his family members, Juan has taken care of himself in ways that will benefit not only himself but the legacy he leaves his children.

Instead of looking to his wife to heal his childhood wounds — and to give him the unconditional love that only a parent can give to a child — Juan has begun taking responsibility for *reparenting* himself. As a boy Juan was not given guidance about various ways one can express anger; as an adult, he has to provide tools and skills to that little boy, in essence becoming responsible for fathering his own childish self. Instead of wallowing in the need for approval he never got, Juan has to find ways to approve of himself.

The responsibility for reparenting the immature, underdevel-oped parts of the self rests squarely on our shoulders; this is both the burden and the opportunity we are all presented with if we choose to explore our family legacies.

Sometimes understanding the many different ways our parents' legacies affect us is easy, for example, when we catch ourselves say-ing something exactly like our father did. At other times we may be blinded to how a legacy affects us. To gain more insight about these connections, and as a way of voicing your intentions to behave dif-ferently than your parents, it may be helpful to discuss your re-sponses to Juan's story, the exercises, or the ideas in this chapter with someone close to you, such as another dad, a friend, or your partner.

CHAPTER 3

Be a New Kind of Provider

'll never forget stepping into the men's bathroom with my friend Nicky at Fenway Park in 1977. I was nine years old, and it was my first Red Sox game without my parents (we lived a mile away). It looked more like an overcrowded stable of bulls than a restroom, and the stench of beer and urine was almost disorienting. I was immediately frightened, first by all the drunk men and then by the realization that there was no organized line to speak of; I would have to fight my way to a urinal. To my horror, Nicky had already begun dodging his way through the crowd. Not wanting to be left alone, I followed him. Moments later, on the other side of this vast room, he stopped next to a trash barrel. I watched in disbelief as he unzipped his pants and began urinating into it. I then looked around and realized men — and now boys — were using not only trash cans and toilets but the row of sinks as well.

Last year I walked into that same men's room in Fenway Park and saw a very different scene. Not only was everyone using the facilities as they were meant to be used — and in a very orderly fashion, I might add — but against the far wall was the big surprise: a diaper-changing station. Even more amazingly, it was being used. The young dad at work was clearly not a novice. He finished quickly but then paused to raise his wide-eyed little one above his head. Just as he brought the baby down and tight to his chest, I watched an older man, without a baby, smile at the young dad and slap him on the back as he passed by. This brief, almost unnoticeable exchange between two men (who clearly didn't know each other) could not have been in greater contrast to what I saw in 1977.

These two indelible snapshots of the men's room in Fenway Park have come to symbolize both how much fatherhood has changed in the past quarter century and the opportunity modern dads have to more fully integrate qualities like caretaking and nurturing into the evolving male identity. *The question is not whether males are capable of embodying these qualities; it's whether we're courageous enough to express them in both private and public life.* If we were to truly start valuing caretaking more as males, the implications could be very far-reaching. We could, for example, raise our voices and insist on making affordable, quality childcare a top priority on the national agenda. Similarly, valuing ourselves as caretakers could alleviate the ridiculous stigma and low wages that prevent more males from going into the helping professions that are so essential to families — early childhood education, social work, and psychology, to name a few. The payoff for raising children who equate caretaking with mom *and* dad, and child-rearing as women's work *and* men's work, is a more realistic, equitable, and rewarding life at home and in the workplace.

My vision is that my son and daughter will grow up to be parents someday and think of themselves not as breadwinners or caretakers but as full providers. We need moms and dads, men and women, who are prepared and willing to provide physically, emotionally, financially, and spiritually for their children. This is not to say that parents can't complement each other at different points in life, or even that any parent, single or not, can or should do it all themselves. We need community; we need each other. However, each of us as parents can begin to think of ourselves as *responsible* for at least having a hand in all these realms — the physical, emotional, financial, and spiritual. In a two-parent family that may mean that one person does the bills but the other understands the overall family financial picture. A single dad with full custody will have to provide in all realms but may, for example, lean on extended family members and a close friend to support meeting his child's emotional needs. Or the live-away dad with partial custody may not get to spend much time with his children but does his best to provide emotionally by staying interested in their daily lives and prioritizing consistent communication with their mother for a fuller picture.

A doctor or a mechanic may have a specialty, but he or she must understand the fundamentals of what makes the whole system — body or automobile — function and thrive.

The Breakdown of the Breadwinner/Caretaker Model

I often feel like I'm mentioning the obvious to parents when I describe how the men's bathrooms in most sports arenas today are equipped with a diaper-changing station. And, as always, a large portion of the women in the audience get a kick out of this factoid. Even many of the men who have older children seem not to have noticed, perhaps because it's still relatively rare to see a diaper change in action. Interestingly, I've also heard from more than a few women at my lectures about the shortage of changing stations in the women's bathrooms at their place of work.

While it may seem mundane or unremarkable, the rather sudden appearance of things baby related in men's bathrooms over the past decade speaks volumes about how modern parenting roles are changing. While dads today may still get some wisecracks (undoubtedly from other men) for changing a diaper at halftime or for sporting the latest baby gear — such as a sling or double-decker stroller — there is, in general, far greater acceptance of men's caregiving role.

Diaper-changing stations did not suddenly appear in men's bathrooms because one day the owners decided that men should share in childcare responsibilities. This is not to say that there haven't always been dads who support equality or dads who've had full custody for their children since birth; however, the changes in parenting roles and responsibilities we're witnessing today are the result of much larger forces that have been at play for decades: changing economic conditions due to globalization, forcing both parents to work; the massive influx of women into all sectors of the workforce, in large part the result of rights gained through the women's movement over the past century; the increasing recognition and acceptance of diverse family structures, the fruit of ongoing struggles in the civil rights and gay and lesbian rights movements; and, perhaps less tangible, the fact that many of America's "latchkey generation" (the children of the first massive wave of divorced parents in the seventies) have become parents over the past decade. All these factors, and many others, have influenced the increasingly significant caretaking role that men are beginning to play in children's lives.

No longer is the male-as-breadwinner/female-as-caretaker model of family life the reality for most Americans. In 2007, 66 percent of married families consisted of dual-income earners; only 33 percent of fathers are the sole wage earners today, versus 51 percent in 1977.[1]

Of course there have always been family structures that have differed from this model. My own grandfather, for example, whose first two wives died during childbirth, raised two of his three daughters for significant periods of time as a single dad. Nor has the breadwinner/caretaker model been a reality for millions of single mothers. Yet schools and most workplaces are still organized in ways that assume every family has a husband who is always available to the employer and a wife totally available to take care of everything else (children, doctor's appointments, elderly family members, etc.).[2]

Increasingly, in two-parent, married families — gay and straight alike — both parents work. According to the 2007 U.S. Census, 66 percent of married couples with children under eighteen had both spouses in the labor force. Strictly in economic terms, women increasingly play the breadwinner role, despite a persistent gender gap when it comes to wages and earnings. We have also begun to see more men, though in far smaller numbers, take on the role of primary caretaker at home or in society in general. As the breadwinner/caretaker model continues to erode — and the roles and responsibilities of who does what in a family become more balanced and fluid — both men and women are forging new identities. One clear manifestation of this for women can be seen in the much publicized (and often sensationalized) "mommy wars," which pit working and stay-at-home mothers against each other in a seemingly irreconcilable battle for the "right way" to mother. Whereas women and mothers have been grappling with identity questions around breadwinning and caretaking for more than a century, men and dads have only just entered the ring.

Despite the fact that modern dads spend more time with their children — by staying at home with them, doing more housework, going to PTA meetings, taking paternity leave — the identity of the modern man is still rooted more in breadwinning than in caretaking.

Men's roles have not kept pace with changing understandings of the desirability of involved fathering: Men are often trapped within narrow gender roles that emphasize work and business, money making, public status and success. It remains difficult for men to genuinely embrace homemaking and childcare without being judged or disapproved of for stepping outside the narrow bounds of masculinity.[3]

In this chapter you will meet dads in different family settings whose stories illustrate the gradual, often difficult integration of caretaking into the modern male identity. Including interviews with wives/partners, this chapter captures some of the central breadwinner/caretaker dilemmas facing modern families, as well as the positive results of trying to be a new kind of provider.

LeWayne Jones, 39

FAMILY: married to Renea Jones; stepdad to a son, sixteen, and a daughter, nineteen, and biological dad to a daughter, twelve
BORN IN: Nashville, Tennessee
LIVES IN: Nashville, Tennessee
OCCUPATION: truck driver

At a recent keynote address I gave at the New England Fathering Conference, I showed a video clip from my interview with LeWayne Jones for the first time. I was very pleased to discover that in the follow-up discussion, the audience of mostly dads and professionals (men and women who work with dads and families) seemed to resonate not only with what LeWayne had to say but with how he said it. Explaining how his wife makes more money than he does, LeWayne endeared himself to the audience — as he did to me when I was first introduced to him through a friend — with his insight, his sincerity, his humility, and his honesty in describing the challenges and rewards of being a new kind of provider. LeWayne, whom you will meet in this chapter and see again in chapter 5, is a fine example of a man on the road from traditional to modern fatherhood.

Leave It to Beaver No More

LEWAYNE: I am a local truck driver. I've got a great schedule. I go in at 6:30 AM and finish by 3:30 PM. My wife owns a hair salon and is a stylist there. We have a weird setup. A lot of guys don't like to say this — and I've kind of gotten over that insecurity — but my wife makes more money than I do. Renea works really hard, usually twelve to fourteen hours a day. We're not the traditional household, because she works so much. I grew up in a house where the man worked as much as he could and provided financially. The woman did the chores. That was my outlook. But in my case, my wife is able to own her own business, and I'm only going to make so much. The roles have changed. I've talked to my dad about it, and he said, "It's different now. Your wife's business is so good, you need to support her as much as you can."

I'm kind of like the mom *and* the dad. I'm not a great cook, but I do cook. I do a lot of the household chores, because my wife stands on her feet all day. She takes the kids to school, and I pick them up. I help with the homework. I do a lot of what we think of as "motherly" things. It's not always comfortable for me, but I have to do it. I've made it a priority to get out of my comfort zone.

One benefit I think my kids get from my wife working more and my being present is it cuts down the stereotype that black dads — and dads in general — aren't involved. My kids get to see a young black father who is involved in their lives in every way. I'm not trying to sound conceited, but I'm around every day. Also, I'm able to implement stuff that my dad wasn't able to because I'm more involved. I couldn't really talk to my father. He did his best, and I think he did a good job, but there was a big emotional part missing. As men, I think we aren't in tune with emotions because we're taught to financially provide; the woman provides the emotion.

I think by nature my wife is in tune with the kids emotionally. If she's been working all day, she comes home and gets involved. By nature, I wouldn't do that. It's difficult for me because I'm not an emotional guy. But now that I'm so involved in the kids' lives, it helps. For example, my daughter, Angel, came home crying because a girlfriend said something mean about her at school. Normally my wife would deal with it, but now I have to. Well, I don't *have* to, but I *want* to because I want the best for her. But it's hard for me because it just wasn't what I was taught. I keep going back to my dad, but I never really saw him deal with our emotional issues — not with my sister, not with my mom, and definitely not with us boys. It was like "suck it up" or "that's just how life is, you gotta move on." So when my daughter would get upset about a bad grade, I used to say things like "it's not a big deal" or "you need to get over that." It took me a while to figure out — actually, I didn't figure it out, my wife had to tell me — that I was shutting her down. I know with my oldest, I shut her down a lot. Things have gotten better since she started college, but I know it affected her. With my two youngest, I've gotten much better.

The "Feminine" Side of the Equation

As mentioned earlier, in addition to the tremendous influx of women into the workforce, the economic realities of family life today (the cost of healthcare, decreased job security, aging parents, etc.) have greatly influenced modern fatherhood. LeWayne is a perfect example of a dad who may not have taken on such an involved role in everyday parenting if not for these new realities. Despite the fact that his wife is financially more successful than he, LeWayne still needs to work full-time as well. That's not to say that if LeWayne were the breadwinner and Renea the primary caretaker, he wouldn't still be a great dad. But this role switch, as LeWayne points out, forces him to step out of his comfort zone. While being on the "motherly" or "feminine" side of the equation — arranging sleepovers, cooking and cleaning, dealing with the emotional roller coaster of his teenage daughter — has its challenges, LeWayne is also aware of how everyone in his family benefits.

Especially given his traditional, patriarchal family upbringing, it would be easy for me to imagine a guy like LeWayne either refusing to take on such a new role or at the very least suffering through it. He could, for example, simply leave his daughter's friendship problems for his wife to deal with after work. This kind of passive stance or inflexibility would, in all likelihood, lead to strife with Renea and would not strengthen his relationship with his daughter. Instead, LeWayne steps up. In the process, he realizes that being involved in the everyday messiness of parenting gives him a golden opportunity to develop the kind of close relationship he wants with his children but never had with his own father. One example of this is LeWayne's involvement in school; not only is he involved in ways his dad was not, but he also sees the opportunity it's given him to build his relationship with his daughter. In the following exercise, LeWayne was asked to rate his own and his father's level of involvement in school. (This topic is addressed in greater depth in chapter 5.)

As you can see on the next page, LeWayne is clearly involved in his children's life at school in ways his dad never was. This exercise is not meant as a criticism of his father or past generations, as the expectations for dads' involvement in schools were very different. It's intended to help you see in bold relief just how much — as in LeWayne's case — or how little has changed.

EXERCISE 6. Assess Your Level of Involvement in Your Child's School: LEWAYNE JONES

I asked LeWayne to use the following scoring system to compare his and his father's involvement at school.

1 = RARELY   2 = SOMETIMES   3 = FREQUENTLY

	YOUR DAD	YOU
Drop off/pick up child	1	3
Parent-teacher conferences	1	3
Volunteer at school	1	2
Parent association meetings	1	2
Parent education events (i.e., speakers)	2	3
Class-level events (i.e., science night)	1	2
Whole-school events (sports, drama, clubs)	1	3
TOTAL	8	18

7 to 11 — You need to do more, get going.

12 to 17 — You're on the right track, keep going.

18 to 21 — You're actively involved, good going.

A Breadwinning Mom and a Stay-at-Home Dad

Like LeWayne's, John Storhm's experience as a modern dad looks nothing like the arrangement he saw growing up. Whereas LeWayne's father was supportive of what must have seemed different, if not downright strange — the wife making more money than the husband — John's father had much more trouble wrapping his head around his son's choice to be a stay-at-home dad. In my interview with John, he recounted his father's reaction: "His response was, 'I don't even know what to call a male nanny.' He was in his seventies at the time and had no idea why I would want to stay home. And there was nothing I could say to make him understand the decision. That was difficult."

Both LeWayne's and John's stories capture as much about the changes in women's lives as about those in men's. What makes them important to the story of modern fatherhood is the way in which each man discovers unforeseen rewards and potential for growth in these modern family arrangements.

John Storhm, 40
FAMILY: married to Kathy Storhm; father of a son, eight
BORN IN: Cleveland, Ohio
LIVES IN: Portland, Oregon
OCCUPATION: stay-at-home dad, computer consultant

In the following section, you will hear not only from John but also from his wife, Kathy. I first met Kathy after a talk I gave at their son's school in Cleveland. John and I corresponded by email a number of times after that lecture. I've included a few excerpts from the email exchange, as well as the interview I did with both of them over the phone.

Role Reversal

JOHN: My wife is a law professor, and I do computer work. We've been moving around for her career since the early '90s. I was teaching computer science and doing some consulting when Kathy got offered a one-year visiting professorship at Cornell University. At the time, we were living in Dayton, Ohio. Soon after she accepted the offer, we found out that Kathy was pregnant and due in the fall — right when her new job was to start. So it was a logical decision that I would be the one to stay home with our son initially.

Staying home was extremely hard to get used to, things like adjusting to his napping and eating schedule. Kathy was breast-feeding, so if I heated up a bottle for his lunch and he wouldn't touch it, then I was out of food. He'd be screaming because he was hungry, so I'd have to drive him to her office. That was very stressful. It was like working for the most unreasonable boss you can imagine.

I have met so many dads who look at me and say, "Man, I would love to be doing what you're doing." I could tell that most of them had no concept of what staying home full-time was really like. They thought it was like a vacation, as if they would get to play sports and have fun with their kid all day long. Most didn't see the work of it at all.

The basic work of being the stay-at-home parent is that you have to completely shift your priorities. It's not about what you want to do; it's about what your child needs you to do. If I have a project that needs to get done around the house, I'm not able to do it because I'm home with my son. I think moms experience it differently than dads; most of the stay-at-home moms I know are "on" 24/7. Not only do they take care of their kids all day, but they also do the whole evening shift because the dads don't turn off their work mode.

The agreement Kathy and I made early on was that when she came home from work, she was expected to be involved. She did not get to kick back and sit on the couch and read the newspaper. She had to spend time with Kele so I could do the stuff I couldn't get to during the day.

Early on, she would come home and do some nursing in the early evening, and we'd have dinner. But as Kele got older and Kathy wasn't breast-feeding anymore, it became harder for Kathy to let go of work when she was at home. Gradually, the work pressures started to impinge on our evenings and weekends. Kathy would play with Kele for a while, and then she'd start to feel like she had to go check email or make a phone call or prepare for a meeting. I think that working parents, male or female, tend to behave the same. Being disconnected from the family is not necessarily the sole domain of men.

KATHY STORHM: I didn't actually take maternity leave — I was back at work six days after Kele was born. John and I didn't really think about what kind of impact all this would have; going straight back to work ended up putting a lot of pressure on me. All of a sudden I felt like, "The responsibility is now mine, I can't screw up, I can't quit, I have to carry the load." Everything needed to be done, and there was a tight schedule, little time, and little money. I think that made me a little more work focused than I would ordinarily have been. Not having had even a month to stay home and relax and kind of get into that groove was problematic in the long run.

Our society doesn't really foster a balanced lifestyle. I think for women, doing it all is not really possible. When I was at work, I was always thinking I ought to be home and spending more time with John and Kele. And when I was home, I was thinking, "I have all this stuff on my desk. I left early and I didn't do this or that." During the workweek it's really difficult because I've got both work and home on my mind all the time, and they both feel like responsibilities I'm supposed to be meeting. But doing it all, whether you're male or female, is simply impossible.

One of my biggest complaints before Kele was that I managed the entire household. I used to refold the laundry that John had folded. It wasn't that he wouldn't help, but I was the one who had to say when it was time to get groceries or when it was time to clean; it was always on my shoulders, and John never owned that responsibility. That switched when he was home all day. I couldn't care less if the floors were dirty in the kitchen.

Trying to work and run a household is difficult for anyone, male or female. I think anyone is a better parent for spending more time with their kids. And so whoever's working outside the home has to balance that. And whoever's working inside the home has to maintain or deal with the frustrations that being at home all day creates. And ultimately, each person tries not to have those things get in the way of the relationship with the child.

Walking a Quarter-Mile in the Other's Shoes

John's experience staying home and being the full-time caretaker for their son was as much of an eye-opener as Kathy's experience as the full-time breadwinner. One obvious conclusion that can be drawn from these short excerpts is that both roles, when the sole responsibility of one person, can be difficult to manage.

As the caretaker, John discovered the awful truth behind the myth so many of us men want to believe — that staying at home and caring for a child is not really "work." Beyond the fact that it calls for a complete reordering of priorities, whereby all of one's wants and needs become secondary, John described how caretaking was also very stressful, like working for "the most unreasonable boss you can imagine." Having stayed home with my daughter for two or three days a week the first year of her life, I could relate to John's experience with other dads who envied his situation. I recall thinking, "If this guy had any idea how difficult it is to be fully responsible for his kid for more then a few hours at a time, he wouldn't be saying how lucky I am." More than anything, this kind of "quaintification" of parenting came across as deluded at best and patronizing at worst. In fact, if more dads walked even a quarter-mile in John's shoes as a full-time stay-at-home dad, it's likely we would have many more family-friendly policies when it comes to paid leave, childcare, and elder care.

Just as John was awakened to the challenges of full-time childcare,

Kathy discovered the dilemma facing the full-time breadwinner. She described how quickly and completely work became her top priority. The line that best captures this transformation is, "I couldn't care less if the floors were dirty in the kitchen." However, it's important to note that despite focusing more on bringing home the bacon, Kathy felt a sense of obligation to be in both places — work and home — at the same time. As mentioned earlier, this internal conflict captures both sides of the "mommy wars." I do believe that dads are increasingly feeling a similar pull, but not necessarily the same sense of obligation, duty, or, as some might say, instinct. In fact, I think the mommy wars could be somewhat alleviated if more dads *did* feel more obligated to balance work and family life. As Kathy points out, our society does not foster such balance for any parents, male or female, married or single, which leaves so many of us trying to do it all.

The reality is that while modern dads are doing more housework and childcare overall, research consistently shows that women (working or not) continue to do the vast majority of housework and child-related tasks.[4] Regardless of who plays what role in the family, dads need to model full participation in home life. In some cases, this may mean that both men and women have to step out of their comfort zones. Remember, children learn what they live. If we don't want our daughters to grow up expecting to do everything at home or our sons to grow up with the idea that participation in family life is optional, then we need to think about what we're modeling.

In the following exercise, which is intended to raise awareness about the division of labor in your family, I asked John to circle who does what in his family in terms of housework and childcare. The idea is to pay attention to the balance of responsibilities and equality between partners. In single-parent families, this exercise can serve as a reminder of different areas where one could focus on finding more support.

EXERCISE 7. **Take a Snapshot of Housework and Childcare Responsibilities in Your Family:**

JOHN STORHM

I asked John to take an inventory of child- and home-related tasks by circling a dot on the following scale.

CHILD-RELATED TASKS	MOSTLY DAD		ABOUT EVEN		MOSTLY MOM
Purchases your children's clothes?	•	•	•	•	⊙
Schedules doctor's appointments?	⊙	•	•	•	•
Makes childcare arrangements?	⊙	•	•	•	•
Bathes and gets younger kids ready for bed?	•	•	•	•	⊙
Arranges social plans such as play dates?	⊙	•	•	•	•
Monitors curfews of older children?	•	•	•	•	⊙
Checks in with your older children?	•	•	⊙	•	•
Sets limits with the children?	•	•	•	⊙	•
Maintains contact with your child's school?	⊙	•	•	•	•

HOUSE-RELATED TASKS	MOSTLY DAD		ABOUT EVEN		MOSTLY MOM
Does the laundry and cleans house?	⊙	•	•	•	•
Takes out the garbage?	•	⊙	•	•	•
Cleans the bathrooms?	•	⊙	•	•	•
Makes lunches?	⊙	•	•	•	•
Makes the beds?	•	•	•	•	⊙
Vacuums and dusts?	⊙	•	•	•	•
Does outside maintenance?	⊙	•	•	•	•
Makes sure the children do their chores?	•	•	•	•	⊙
Does the food shopping?	⊙	•	•	•	•
Cooks family meals?	⊙	•	•	•	•
Cleans up after family meals?	⊙	•	•	•	•
Does the finances?	•	⊙	•	•	•
Buys gifts and writes thank-you notes?	⊙	•	•	•	•

I Want to Be a Stay-at-Home Dad When I Grow Up

JOHN: Raising a boy and being a stay-at-home dad breaks down a lot of gender stereotypes from the beginning. Kele never had the sense that working was a man thing and that staying home was a woman thing. He saw me home every day, and Kathy going to work, so he already had an untraditional view of gender roles. It wasn't until he got to preschool that he came home and said, "Men are supposed to work." That was the first time he had come in contact with the traditional roles. Then in first grade — he had a writing assignment about what he wanted to be when he grew up — he told us he wanted to be a stay-at-home dad.

KATHY: I think all kids need connection, they need nurturing, and they're happy to give it back. Those behaviors are innate. We have to stop doing the damage we do to boys and girls by forcing them into these stereotypes and saying, "We don't value caring behaviors in boys; we value them in girls." And then we don't value girls as highly because we don't see nurturing behavior as valuable.

I think Kele has a really close relationship with both of us that might have been harder to achieve if we had followed gender stereotypes. If John wasn't who he is, and was a more traditional guy, he wouldn't have had the same close relationship with him. And Kele values the choice that John's made and the impact it's had on his life. He wants to do the same thing for his kids when he grows up. I think that's phenomenal.

Helping Boys See Themselves as Future Dads

My four-year-old son, Jake, recently informed me that he was, in fact, also a daddy, just like me. As part of our nightly ritual, we lay together on his bed, he rolls over, I scratch his back, and then I tell a story. One night, somewhere after the back-scratch, I noticed that Jake was quietly petting his little stuffed swan — aptly named Swanny.

I quietly said, "You're *really* good at taking care of Swanny." He told me that Swanny was his baby and that he was his daddy. "What makes someone a *good* daddy?" I asked. He responded promptly with a list, "They feed the baby, keep it warm, take care of the baby when it's sick."

Then Jake asked me if *I* had ever been a baby. When I told him I had, he switched from petting Swanny to petting my face and said in his little voice, "If you were a baby, I would give you hugs and kisses. I would be so gentle." As he's saying this, the back of his tiny hand is resting on my cheek.

A few days after the spontaneous fatherhood forum with Jake, I had a profound realization: I could not think of a single time when my father, stepfather, or any other adult males had ever talked with me about fatherhood — how being a dad had changed them, what mistakes they promised not to repeat, what qualities it takes to be a dad, or how I would make a great father someday.

Thinking about this exchange with Jake also helped clarify an important step we modern dads must take with our kids in this convergence of identities and manhood. I believe we need to raise our boys to value qualities like care, tenderness, nurturing, and empathy not only by modeling but also by talking about our experiences. Boys need to hear our stories.

Most of us while growing up saw a model of fatherhood that took some form of absence and distance, whether that was because Dad was busy providing and worked a lot or because he opted out of marriage and parenting altogether and left. The reality is that everyone's father — even if he wasn't around much — has a story about fatherhood, about bringing a child into this world, and being responsible, or losing his way, about his dreams for his kids, about the past and future legacy. Boys desperately need these stories to begin crafting their own narratives about fatherhood.

Like so many dads today, I never heard much of my father's story. I knew he loved me, I knew teaching me sports was important to him, I knew he worked hard in an office building, and I knew he liked to drink and had a very short fuse. I didn't know what being a dad was like for him or what his dad was like. All I had were my little-boy observations.

There was a generational silence that left many of us feeling as if we were just supposed to take everything as it came, to find our own way. We were taught that there was something wrong if we couldn't figure it out, even if "it" was something as life changing as becoming a dad. There was no story line to follow, few characters to emulate, and very little sense of the skills we'd need for the job. This lack of narrative is one of the reasons many dads today feel like we're making it up, working in a void, beating our own path. I do not want Jake and his generation of boys to endure or tolerate another generation of men's silence, absence, or distance. Boys need to see and hear the story of fatherhood over the course of their childhoods — what it means to be a good dad today, why caretaking and nurturance are essential qualities to develop, how important it is to communicate with the child's other parent.

Ultimately, I want Jake to have a language with which to tell his own story of fatherhood — what he learned about it growing up, what being a dad meant to his father (me), and eventually what being a dad (or dad figure) means to him. One way or another, our children, especially our sons, will have a story about fatherhood. The question is, Will we equip them with the words and actions to make it a meaningful story that will evolve with each future generation, or will the story be cloaked in silence? This generational legacy of silence, the untold story of fatherhood, must stop now.

Women have been thinking, writing, and talking about what motherhood means for generations. Research, literature, a political legacy, a cultural imagery, and most important, an oral tradition gets passed from mothers to daughters — though not always in healthy ways, and it is not always a happy story. My daughter had a working definition of what a mother is and does from a very young age, which she verbalized and demonstrated in her imaginative doll play.

If we don't teach boys to value caretaking qualities — whether in the working world or in family life — how will they become strong and loving dads? How will they stay physically and mentally healthy if they don't know how to ask for help? How will they build healthy relationships if they don't have the courage to be vulnerable? How will they learn how to support their spouse or partner in the working world if they know little about life in the home? Boys need to see men who are strong and bighearted, tough and tender.

Daughters need caretaking dads no less than sons do. If they are to grow up expecting to be treated respectfully, equally, and lovingly by the boys and men in their lives, girls need to experience such behavior from the important adult men — their dads and dad figures — in their lives as well.

MORE MODERN DADS: **Respecting Daughters' Voices**

Brad Kofoed, 44
FAMILY: married; father of three daughters, eight, six, and four
BORN IN: Denver, Colorado
LIVES IN: Walnut Creek, California
OCCUPATION: entrepreneur, business owner

BRAD: Last night, I walked in and my little girl told me that she didn't like it when I told her not to cry on the sports field. One of the relics of my own boyhood experience was when you fall down on the court or field, you get up, brush yourself off, and keep playing — even if it hurts. My immediate instinct was to get defensive and tell my daughter, again, all the reasons why it's important not to cry and, essentially, why I'm right.

Fortunately, my wife, Tamara, was right there to step in. "Brad," she said, "she's practiced saying this to you a lot of times."

I was floored. The fact that my daughter had to be completely rehearsed and prepared for fear of retribution or how I might react to her honesty was not easy for me to hear. It's a pretty bad indictment of the kind of environment I've created. But I'm glad it came up. I needed to be able to hear that and make some changes.

This incident really goes to the core of my own personal work, my challenge: being a better listener and making sure I'm approachable. That doesn't mean I concede every viewpoint or my principles, but that no matter what I want to communicate, I respect my daughter's viewpoint as well.

What I've found incredibly important — and validating to my daughters — is also learning to say I'm sorry. The idea of apologizing to a four-year-old for my parenting was completely foreign to me. However well intentioned, communication with my own dad was much more about "this is the way it is" or "you should think or feel this way," and not "how do you see things, son?" Apologizing to a child for something he said or did as a parent would not have occurred to him; like many men of his generation, he was head of the household so his view was basically always right.

The presumption I used to have is that I'm the parent, I make the rules around here, the parent is generally right, and the child learns from the parent. The fear was that if I exposed my weakness as a father — by saying I made a mistake — then

I would be teaching my kids not to listen to me. I now know that logic is flawed. The flaw is that if they listen to me because I'm the father and I'm always right, the relationship is based on power, whereas if they're listening to me because *they know that I will truly listen to their perspective and let my guard down*, that is a more powerful conversation, an actual dialogue.

I'm trying hard to be a better communicator and not just listen enough to rebut what's being said, but actually listen to what's being said to me. If I'm not paying attention or being dismissive of my daughters' point of view, I could easily miss out on the impact I'm having on them.

Double Standards

KATHY: For many women who either presume that they have to stay home or think that they want to, the reality of motherhood is often different from what we have in our heads. We develop these pictures of motherhood when we're in middle school of how fun and wonderful it will be; the reality of parenting, especially parenting in this culture, makes this ideal very difficult to achieve.

JOHN: The advantage of being the stay-at-home dad, as opposed to a stay-at-home mom, is that it's completely valid for me to say, "Not only have I lost my identity, but I'm not so happy about it either!" I have the freedom to talk with Kathy about being unhappy, and we can then make the necessary adjustments. Moms are supposed to be happy to give up their careers and take on the responsibilities of childcare. This makes it very hard for the stay-at-home moms to say, "This isn't fulfilling," because they're supposed to find fulfillment in this role. I believe this has a lot to do with why so many moms get postpartum depression, because the traditional gender setup dictates that you shouldn't be unhappy or unfulfilled at this time in your life.

There's very little recognition of the fact that in today's society both parents generally need to work to maintain a household. These days one salary, as most single parents know, is hard to get by on. The assumption in most workplaces, even in Kathy's job, is that someone (typically, the mom) is home to take care of the children. Kathy has to go to meetings, go away to conferences, go out to dinner, be on conference calls, and do all this stuff to maintain her job, and childcare cannot impinge on that.

If Kele is home from school on a snow day or if he gets sick, even the school district assumes that somebody is going to be home to take care of him. The same is true for aging parents who need to be taken care of. This is something that gets completely ignored by most sectors of the working world. Finding even part-time work with the kind of flexibility a parent needs is next to impossible. And if you do find such a job, with the cost of childcare, you might end up actually losing money.

I think the biggest change we need to make is to have paid parental leave. You shouldn't have to jeopardize your salary or your position in order to stay home with your child. I also think it would be really good for each person in a relationship to be able to stay home for six months or even a year after a child is born. Even though it would be great for both parents to stay home at the same time, switching it so that each parent is home for a certain amount of time would help more dads understand the caretaking role much better.

Coparenting

In a better world, the workplace would be more aligned with the realities of family life, as John describes. Though not perfect, the idea of encouraging paternity leave is a good one and one that many European countries have already begun implementing. In Sweden, Norway, and Iceland, for example, policy makers have introduced a "use it or lose it" paternity leave, available only for the man to take — he can't transfer it to his partner.[5] Fathers in Sweden spend more time with their young children than do those of any other nation in the developed world.

While some American companies actually do offer paternity leave, very few men take it. The reasons for this have mostly to do with a fear that they will be seen as less committed to the company and will therefore miss out on advancement opportunities. Less tangible, but no less salient, is the stigma that men fear will be attached to them for choosing childcare over work. Childcare isn't yet considered "manly" behavior. In her testimony before Congress about the changing workplace, Ellen Galinsky of the Families and Work Institute summed up what needs to change for both men and women at work: "Workplaces need to provide flexible career options for the one in four women who want to take time out of the workforce when they have children and the provision of on-ramps that enable them to sequence back to work. These options also need to include fathers and others who need leaves when they have teenagers, elder care responsibilities, compassion care responsibilities and so forth."[6]

In the final section of this chapter, you will meet Ted and Derek, two dads whose approach to parenting, while on the face of it looks like a traditional breadwinner/caretaker model, is quite unique.

Derek Peake, 44, and Ted Uno, 39
FAMILY: married; foster dads to three boys, ages fifteen,
   thirteen, and eight, and two girls, eight and six
BORN IN: Derek, Honolulu, Hawaii;
   Ted, Oakland, California
LIVE IN: Oakland, California
OCCUPATION: Derek, stay-at-home dad; Ted, lawyer

When I first met Ted and Derek about fifteen years ago, they were in the beginning stages of adopting their first child, Nicholas. Just before the adoption became legally official, I had begun searching for subjects to participate in my documentary *All Men Are Sons:*

Exploring the Legacy of Fatherhood. After talking with Ted and Derek about the project, they agreed to be in the film. For the next three years I was given full access to their journey into fatherhood, which included adopting another son, Javier, and a vision of a larger family. Having known them as passionate, committed, and unbelievably hard-working educators for social justice, it came as little surprise that they would embody these same qualities as dads. Over the course of filming and in the years afterward, I watched as they consciously built a stable, consistent, and loving home.

Last year, I asked if I could interview them for this book. When I arrived at their home, again, I saw that their vision had become reality: they were fostering a baby girl, with the full intention to adopt, as well as a young brother and sister, who were in serious need of committed, loving, and consistent parenting. No longer running the successful youth leadership organization they cofounded, Ted had become a child advocate lawyer and Derek a stay-at-home dad.

DEREK: I think what we do really well with the kids is put them first. We are committed to spending time with them and to restructuring and rethinking how best to support them. It's our commitment to ourselves — it's what we most want in our lives — and it's our commitment to them.

I am now officially the stay-at-home dad. I am the person who controls the schedule and figures out what's needed to run the household. So if anything, I am the nurturer. But it's not "can't we all just get along?"; it's more like "what does it take for us to get along?" I come up with these solutions in the family. Ted is what you would call the breadwinner.

TED: At work, I'm an attorney. I have fun and like what I do and hope we're doing some good, but there isn't a lot of "being nice" involved in my work. The energy is pure attack; you're at war. My job is to push to the point of breaking. That's what I do, that's what I'm paid to do. I can't say to my clients, "They seemed sad so I didn't push them anymore."

My challenge is that you simply can't bring that kind of ferocity home with you. It's detrimental to your kids. So shifting gears emotionally, but somehow remaining present both at home and at work, can be really difficult.

Recently I've been working a lot, and I mean a *lot*. So my challenge has really been to be fully present. And I don't just mean physically being there — though that's been a challenge too — I mean being able to let go of other things, not tensing up or having my head someplace else working out a problem.

DEREK: We set boundaries with ourselves, we set boundaries with the kids, and we're transparent about them. So the kids don't feel abandoned when Ted's at work. They don't feel like, "Oh, we miss Ted"; instead it's more like, "He works so we get to have these opportunities." That way when we're all together we're much more celebratory. We also think of our parenting in terms of an investment strategy, with a short and long term. The kids understand that Ted, in doing his part for the family, makes these other things possible. This is part of the fabric of our family.

We construct the ebb and flow of our parenting so that Ted is a full partner. So I don't consider myself the "primary parent." I'm just the more accessible, stay-at-home parent. Ted and I coparent our kids. There's not a decision that I would make without Ted being fully invested in it. And except for rare moments, we have dinner together every night as a family.

TED: I love how Derek creates that space for me, and he doesn't see me, being the breadwinner and the one not as accessible, as any less valuable. He holds me accountable when I'm not holding up my end, which is great. When you're totally immersed in work it's easy to kind of say, "This hurts to not be physically present with my family, so I'll just close off and focus fully on my work so I won't feel the pain." It's a lot easier to close yourself off, but it's just not the right thing to do.

Instead, I really recognize that my family is allowing me to work this hard. There is no way I could do any of what I'm doing without them supporting me and being present in my life. On a practical level, without Derek doing everything he does every day at home, there's no way I could bring focus to my work. If he weren't holding down the fort and going to all the appointments, how could I be focused? The sense of fulfillment that I have, the energy the family gives me, allows me to achieve at a level that I wouldn't ordinarily be able to. They are the reason I do the work that I do.

DEREK: Ted also sacrifices a lot of his personal space. So it's not as if his workday ends and he can have dinner, do homework with the kids, and then do the bedtime routines. It means he does all that and then resumes working at 9:00 PM until 2:00 AM, then he wakes up at 7 AM and works until dinner again. He's just changed the ways in which he gets in his twelve to fourteen hours of work a day, while not having it detract from family time. But he's willing to do that. He breaks his momentum to put that family time first.

A New Model

Although Ted and Derek's arrangement might look strikingly similar to a traditional breadwinner/caretaker setup, their approach to these roles is unique. Despite having somewhat prescribed roles — Ted works long hours and financially provides, while Derek manages the kids' daily schedules and routines — there is what they describe as an ebb and flow, or a fluidity, to these roles. Ted and Derek are supportive of each other and go to great lengths to make sure their children understand the different ways each prioritizes and contributes to the family unit. By being transparent about who does what and why, they not only model values such as cooperation, sacrifice, and love but also provide a more realistic picture of adult life and parenthood. Conversely, many of us avoid going into much detail about our roles and responsibilities, resorting to simple explanations or nonstarters like, "Daddy goes to work so he can make money for the family and we can have a roof over our head."

Ted and Derek hold each other accountable for fulfilling their respective roles. This kind of power sharing is unique in that neither dad is master of his respective domain and subordinate to the other's; historically, in the traditional heterosexual arrangement, these domains would often break down along stereotypical gender lines. For instance, if the woman was master of the domestic domain, the man would likely know very little about where to buy the kids' clothes or how to bake a casserole for ten. If the man brought in the sole income, he would likely have ultimate control over the distribution of money in the family, leaving the woman in the subordinate position of having to acquiesce to his wishes or demands.

CHAPTER 4

Find Balance through Ritual

"What are your top priorities at this point in your life?" I asked the sizable group of dads in a high school auditorium. "What matters most to you?" I then warned them that my follow-up question was a bit more macabre and perhaps too close to home for some but nonetheless important to consider. "Now, imagine many, many years have passed and your time has come, your number is up, it is your final hour — however you want to put it." A few guys chuckled awkwardly. I then asked the group to try to put themselves there with an image, thought, or feeling. The room quickly went quiet. "In your final, peaceful hour, what do you imagine would occupy your mind, your heart? What would you be thinking about?"

I could almost hear the gears turning. Before anyone could speak, I interrupted the pensive crowd: "My guess is that not a single one of you, in that final hour, would be wishing you'd spent more time, or been more attentive to, or savored every moment of every day — at work." This time the chuckles were louder and the heaviness that had begun to fill the room quickly lifted. "Every man in this room knows exactly what would consume our hearts and minds in that final hour." As I paused again, the jokers and wise guys in the room, amazingly, left this perfect moment alone.

"So, if in the end, it really is all about our children, about the people we love, about our *relationships*, the question is, How much of our time and true presence do they get from us? Where else do we spend our minutes, hours, and days on any given week?"

What Are Your Priorities?

The pace of modern life and the demands of making a living (and the accompanying stress) are commonly cited by dads as the main roadblocks to truly prioritizing children and family. As we saw in chapter 3, scarcity of time is a pervasive problem for both moms and dads, whether parents work, stay at home, or do both. Balancing work and home, doing it all (especially for single parents), is made increasingly difficult without workplace policies to match the realities of parenting. Also, in our mobile society, many parents lack the support of a community or extended family. As my friend Ethan once said, "It feels like it's me and my wife against the world."

When I ask any dad about his priorities, almost without fail it's his children, his family. However, when we put our lives under a microscope and ask ourselves difficult questions such as, "What does success *really* mean to me?" often a different story about priorities becomes clear. Most of us, at various points in our lives, find discrepancies — some small, some huge — between what we say our priorities are and what we really do. And at times, when we're being less than honest with ourselves or when we lose our way, it's often our loved ones who give us the message that we must restore balance. A comprehensive study by the Work and Family Institute found that children today are most concerned with how stressed out their parents are, which is certainly a reminder to step back and take stock.[1]

In this chapter, you will meet two dads who are seeking to close the gap between saying they prioritize family and actually doing it. Along the way, each man shares not only times when his life has fallen out of balance but also practical ways he has repaired his family relationships. In the first story you will be reintroduced to Bobby Lee Smith, whom I described briefly in chapter 2, a dad who learns some difficult but ultimately enlightening lessons about the importance of slowing down. His is a cautionary tale that powerfully shows how falling out of balance can not only exact a heavy price on the family but also be a matter of life and death.

Bobby Lee Smith, 53

FAMILY: married; father of a daughter, fourteen
BORN IN: Washington, Georgia
LIVES IN: Nashville, Tennessee
OCCUPATION: CEO and president of the Boys and Girls
    Clubs of America/Eastern Tennessee

When I first met Bobby, he seemed a man of few words. I had just finished speaking at the first dads' dinner at his daughter's school in Nashville. He waited until I'd finished answering questions, signing books, and saying goodnight to others before approaching me. I can usually tell when this kind of event truly hits home with a dad; in Bobby's case, I could tell from his very quiet, thoughtful, and deliberate way of approaching me. He didn't even ask a question; he just wanted me to know that he'd appreciated the talk and that it'd gotten him thinking about his own dad.

I could tell there was a story there. When I finally sat down with Bobby in Nashville, months after the talk at his daughter's school, I knew almost nothing about his story. Within minutes of listening to him, it was clear that my hunch was right. Bobby Lee's was an epic tale.

The Wear and Tear of Work

BOBBY: I traveled every week out of town for about ten years. Prior to a major leadership change, it was a pretty rigid work culture. If you went out of town on Monday and you got back on Friday at 2:00 PM, rather than go home, you'd go to the office. Being in and out of airports, resolving crises in the various communities I worked in, made it a very stressful job. Making sure things got done, taking care of the people around me at work, and burning the candle at both ends often left my body running on fumes. It's a state of mind in which you're confused, but you're not aware of the confusion and the impact that you're having on others.

Family was not top priority — it was more like second or third. In fact, it seemed like I was fighting against my family. I was high-strung and short-tempered — kind of in a different zone altogether — when it came to relating to my wife and daughter. They would ask me something, and I would get annoyed and give knee-jerk reactions. My wife would constantly talk to me about my tone, saying things like, "Bobby, did you hear how you said that?" I would deny it. My pride would get in the way of admitting things or apologizing.

Gradually, the general wear and tear of work left me feeling that a connection to my family and to my spirituality was missing. I would come home on a Friday after traveling and then be focused on doing stuff for church and for other people over the weekend. When I looked at the amount of time I was spending engaged in meaningful conversation with my wife and daughter, or finding out what was going on in their lives, I realized how little we were connecting.

I wasn't happy and started to feel like I wasn't involved in my daughter's life, just as my own dad had missed out on my life growing up. "You need to be there for Bree. Your dad wasn't there, and you don't want to be like that" kept coming up for me over and over again.

I felt like I was stuck and like the only two things I knew how to do were traveling and working. So when a job opportunity to work more locally in New Orleans came up I saw it as the way back to being a family and a way for me to stop traveling. Not only did the job require minimal travel, but it would bring us closer to my wife's family in Louisiana.

In July 2005 my wife moved to Atlanta to finish her doctorate in divinity at Emory, and Bree and I moved to New Orleans. This time for Bree and me to connect as father and daughter, we decided, would be good for everyone. My wife would join us once a month on the weekend.

Katrina hit a month after we arrived.

After we moved back into New Orleans, there were no services, nowhere to get your hair cut, get your clothes cleaned, or get something to eat. Some of the fast-food restaurants started to open up, but they were cash only. Many of the basic things you take for granted every day, like ATMs or televisions, just weren't there.

Coming back into that devastated environment and then trying to be a single dad — I considered myself a single dad during that time because my wife was in Atlanta that whole year — was a totally new experience. Making sure that Bree was prepared for school and that she got there each day, as well as handling my job — rebuilding five Boys and Girls Club sites — was incredibly stressful.

In the evening when Bree was at home, I was laying a lot of expectations on her — you need to do your homework, make sure you clean your room, and so on — and generally not being sensitive to her state of mind in all of the transition. At one point, she just broke down crying, saying how unfair I was being; the more she tried to share her feelings and where she was coming from, the angrier I got. Once again, this had everything to do with me not taking care of myself and being too stressed out. Katrina just made everything worse.

Losing Sight of What Matters

It's amazing how many dads I talk to realize the toll that work is taking on them and yet do nothing to change it. Whether it's because we've worked so hard to get where we are or because working less or in a different capacity seems impossible for economic or other reasons, for many dads change is hard to come by. As one who struggles with balance myself, I draw inspiration from other dads — some are close friends, and others, like Bobby and the other dads in this book, I meet along the way — who are mindfully trying to keep their values in line with their daily realities.

Like Bobby, sometimes we lose sight of what's important. When I get so wrapped up in my pursuits at work and have difficulty even imagining a life with less travel — the irony of my speaking to a group of dads about engaged fatherhood while three thousand miles from my home is rarely lost on me — I turn to the story of a close friend who mustered the courage to turn away from a lucrative career loaded with perks to be a stay-at-home dad. Another dad I met in a workshop had a simple rule, which I work hard to follow: he stops working, no matter what, at 5:30 every night so he can be home for dinner.

For some, gradual change is more realistic and fruitful than taking a radical approach to a balanced work and family life. However, more wholesale change, as Bobby's story later reveals, is sometimes the only path. In his seminal work *I Don't Want to Talk about It*, my friend and colleague Terry Real describes how in some cases workaholism can be masking a *covert depression*.[2] In other words, to ward off depression — a disease that breaks all the rules of traditional masculinity about being tough and without needs — some men will pour themselves into their work. This is not to say that every man who works hard is depressed. I do think that it is a valuable question — whether you are really depressed under all that busyness — to ask if you find yourself working all the time with no time for family, or anything else.

Waking Up to What Matters

BOBBY: It finally reached a point where I realized things were not right. My anger became a red flag. I managed to tone myself down and really force myself to respond in a different way to Bree.

I also spent a lot of time at church in New Orleans, praying and reading the Bible. I know that helped elevate me to a different level where I was able to start putting everything into perspective.

We survived our eighteen months in New Orleans and moved back to Nashville. Soon after returning, I had my yearly physical exam, and my doctor noticed that I had elevated sugar levels. He told me to watch what I was eating and to continue exercising. I guess I had gotten caught up in the excitement of moving, had stopped exercising, and had put on some weight.

I recently found out the hard way that I'm a type 2 diabetic. In a period of three weeks, I lost about eighteen pounds and was experiencing all the symptoms and was in a state of denial.

Sometimes you have to get hit across the head with something — physically or mentally — before you wake up and focus on what really needs your attention. I see Katrina almost like my diabetes: they were both wake-up calls saying, *"You need to get it right."* I've *had* to shift my priorities so that I'm taking care of myself, my health, and my family — the things that should come first anyway.

I've also made communication with my daughter a higher priority. When Briana was about five or six, my wife would go into her room, sit down, and spend time just allowing her to talk. At the time I just didn't see myself doing those "motherly" or "girly" things. Now I see that by allowing Bree to share whatever she wanted, uninhibited, my wife was really setting the stage for lifelong communication.

I've missed a lot of these kinds of opportunities with Bree. There were those fifteen or twenty minutes on the drive to school, before she hit her teens, when she would talk about the little things with me. That changed right around twelve or thirteen. Then her talk became more about relationships and issues she was having with friends, things I thought she should be talking to her mother about. I should have been connecting more and listening more.

Now I'm much more focused on making sure the conversation is happening, at least to some degree, on that level. In one of our recent conversations on the way to school, Bree told me about a dream in which she was artificially inseminated! She's fourteen, and

I'm sitting there listening and really thinking, "What! Artificially inseminated!" I was ready to go into lecture mode, but then I caught myself and said, "No just allow her to express herself." So she took me through the whole dream, how the baby was taken away after it was born and how sad she was, and all this stuff. At the end of the story, I just said, "Briana, thank you for sharing."

"Mothering" is a natural instinct for women, but I think that fathers have the same instinct. Being the father of a daughter, I have the same natural instinct to do some of the "feminine" things my wife does, such as cooking, stroking Bree's hair, caring for her. Societal roles distract us from doing those things — I look at the way my job took me away and became more important than my family.

Recently Bree told me her stomach hurt. She lay down beside me, and I simply put my arms around her. That was all it took. Fifteen minutes later she felt better and went back upstairs to her room. Now, that's what I call being a dad.

Getting It Right

None of us wants to get to the point where illness, divorce, or some other tragedy awakens us to the importance of slowing down. Bobby's story is as cautionary as it is inspiring. Despite the seductiveness of thinking you will be happy *when*... or things will be better *if*... or I will change *after*... there is no time like the present to slow down and pay attention to what matters most.

As I'm writing this, my wife's stepfather, Jack — better known to our children as "gramps" — is recovering from surgery after being diagnosed with stage 2 cancer of the appendix only weeks ago; my own stepfather, Dave (aka Boppa), goes in for heart surgery next month. Within a month's time, our family has had to face the prospect — try as we do, to be optimistic — of a world without two of the most important men in our lives. Having the chance to watch these two men's hearts blossom in the presence of our children has been one of the greatest gifts any parent could wish for. But, of course, we all want more.

Like Bobby Lee Smith, both Gramps and Boppa are warning lights and beacons for millions of dads today. All three men have realized what and who is most important in their lives and have set their priorities accordingly. Yet each man has also lived many years, for varying reasons and at different life stages, out of balance. With the scales tipped to work, not home; to head, not heart; and to silence, not expression, many modern dads, myself included, are heedlessly living unbalanced lives. Things need not be so.

Bobby's story so poignantly captures the simple pleasures any dad can enjoy when we "get it right." Before his awakening, he would have viewed his daughter complaining about her stomach hurting as a drain on his time. How often do we, like Bobby, forget that our children's desire for attention — no matter how it's communicated — is not only an opportunity but a blessing we are lucky to receive?

Some of us fear that giving our children time and attention will somehow divert our eyes from the prize of being a good enough provider; others, like Bobby, are afraid we won't know how to give our children what they need and hide behind the mistaken belief we learned growing up that it's not our job anyway. In other words, it is often out of fear that we tip the scales in the wrong direction. In those moments — like this morning, when Jake wrapped his arms around my legs as I tried to get out the door to get to work — we have to remember that the health of our children, our family, and ourselves is hanging in the balance.

Quite often after I finish speaking, someone approaches me with a suggestion or idea. Sometimes I am presented with a real gem. On one such occasion, after I had spoken at a dad's breakfast event in a school cafeteria, a dad shared a handful of what my father called kernels of wisdom. First he quoted Gandhi: "Learn something as if it's forever. Do something as if you'll die tomorrow." Then he encapsulated some teachings of Indian philosopher Jiddu Krishnamurti, who said that we need to

1. Reflect on why we do what we do.
2. Find a balance between having no self-awareness and over-thinking everything.
3. Find a balance between letting our history inform us and letting that history limit us.

Indeed, achieving balance is at the heart of solving the modern dad's dilemma. When we're pulled in multiple directions, we have to respond with intention and creativity. One of the most effective ways to find balance is through rediscovering or creating rituals and routines we can rely on when facing too many demands on our time.

Creating Balance through Ritual and Routine

What follows is the story of one father's way of weaving ritual and routine into the fabric of family life and into his relationship with his sons. Through ritual and routine, he is able to maintain a balance between a busy work life as a CEO of a multimillion-dollar company with an equally active and demanding home life. The following story is of a young dad making use of lessons learned.

Dusty Ebers, 31
FAMILY: married to Amy Ebers; father of three sons, six, three, and ten months
BORN IN: Mill Valley, California
LIVES IN: Piedmont, California
OCCUPATION: CEO of Karen Neuberger, Inc.

At one point during my search for dads to interview for this book, I wanted to talk with a CEO who was head of a company with progressive work-life balance policies; of course, I imagined, he would also be the living embodiment of those policies in his own daily life. Admittedly, for the sake of structure and time, I did my best to describe in some detail the exact story I was looking for. This would allow me to most efficiently match up the ideas and activities I wanted to write about with stories of dads who both illustrated and illuminated what I had to say. It didn't take long for me to realize that no matter how nicely I imagined the pieces fitting together, it never worked out that way. Without fail, the interviews always yielded new discoveries that shone different light on what I had to say.

I was introduced to Dusty through another dad in the book. With all the preconceptions about how busy a CEO of a sizable company would be, I was surprised by how flexible, responsive, and personable Dusty was on the phone. In my mind, I thought I'd get to know his assistant better than him (now that I think of it, I didn't ever talk to an assistant). More important, upon arriving at his home to do our interview, I was introduced to his wife, Amy. Similarly accommodating, she agreed on the spot to do an interview after I finished with Dusty. I explained the somewhat uncomfortable truth of my process: interviewing spouses/partners not only enriches a story but allows me to get some corroboration. Dusty and Amy didn't bat an eye.

The Ritual of Shabbat

AMY: Our life has been really hectic the past few years. We've moved a lot, had babies, difficult pregnancies, work stress . . . we've had a lot of different things. But on Friday night, we have our family dinner together and the Jewish day of rest, the Sabbath, begins. The Sabbath begins at sundown on Friday night and lasts until sundown on Saturday night — a total of twenty-five hours. When everything else is crazy and you have no idea what's going to happen the six other nights or days during the week, just knowing that Friday night we are all going to be together — nobody will be on the cell phone or computer — is really, really special. It's very centering to know that even if Dusty's traveling or been working every night, he will get home on Friday night and for the next day he will be present in our family time. Now it's something we're all very committed to as a family. It's about creating time together while at the same time incorporating Jewish traditions that have been around for thousands of years.

DUSTY: My wife and I were both raised Jewish. As I got older, and because I had lived in Israel a few different times during and after college, I realized that I wanted to have a more traditional home and to have our children experience the richness of our Jewish customs and traditions. We also looked at the breakdown of a lot of families in America and could see that with crazy work schedules and other commitments, families (including ours) were running in every direction. Yet so much of our history, our culture, and our heritage was deeply rooted in bringing the family closer together.

We looked back to our grandparents' generation, when they couldn't even put food on the table, and saw that the Jewish traditions and culture in their backgrounds were very strong. They came to America with nothing in terms of material things, but they had a wealth of knowledge and culture. Our parents' generation, through the whole process of making a life in America and assimilating, was not as fully committed to Judaism as our grandparents' generation. So we were really trying to bring it back out of respect for our grandparents, our great-grandparents, and so on.

Our generation, especially those who are now the second generation of Holocaust survivors, has reached a pivotal point. Many families today are educated and in the middle to upper classes; as a group of people, a lot of these families — not all, of course — have gained tremendous professional success. Unfortunately, for some, that comes with losing a little bit of our tradition, our heritage, and our culture, along the way. From a generational standpoint, if my wife and I are not committed to carrying on the traditions, then the chances of our children marrying and raising their kids Jewish are slim to none.

Ritual is at the center of Judaism. The concept of Shabbat, the Sabbath or "the day or rest," is a time that we as a family can be together. It's really helped bring our family together. It's become a tremendous backbone for our family life.

On Friday night we have Shabbat dinner. Sometimes we go to friends' houses, and other times we have friends or family come over. Recently, though, our favorite Friday nights are spent alone as a family. We first do a "children's dinner" and have them recite the prayers they have learned at school over wine (grape juice for the kids) and challah bread and sing the songs they have been practicing. At dinner, we talk about something that was really exciting, something that each of the kids loved doing that day or during the week. Our oldest likes to go through the portion of the Torah he's learned at school for the week (which is also read at synagogue on Saturday) and to talk about that at dinner. Then we get the kids to bed early and have a relaxing adult dinner, just the two of us. After dinner, we catch up on our reading and talk about the week.

On Saturday we just hang out in the morning. I usually take our two older boys to synagogue — Amy sometimes brings the baby a little bit later — which is about a fifteen-minute walk from our house. When I was younger I didn't really like going to synagogue, but our kids love going.

The routine is a big piece of it, and they get to see their friends, and there are activities for them. Amy and I also see friends and acquaintances whom we know in the community. Then we either go directly home, inviting friends to have lunch with us, or we'll have lunch with friends at their house. Depending on when everybody gets back from synagogue, lunch usually starts around one or two and ends up going right through to an early dinner for the kids. There are many nights when it's seven or eight o'clock before we all get home. We put the kids into bed, and then Amy and I usually have time together on Saturday night or get a babysitter and go out.

We explain to our kids that some Jewish families do more, and others do less in terms of rituals. We teach them that there's no right and wrong; it's just whatever works for each individual family. Of course they also meet kids who aren't Jewish and have other types of rituals.

Another thing I've found very helpful in balancing work and family commitments is coaching sports. I've coached my oldest in T-ball and soccer. Not only is coaching a commitment to my son, but it's also a commitment to all his friends and the other parents.

Can I pinpoint exactly what effect I'm having on my boys? No, but I know that I'm an active participant in their development. I'd be remiss if I didn't also say that Amy does an incredible job with the three of them. She is the backbone of our family. As a family unit we're very strong and very tight. I feel that with each of the three boys, we have a wonderful connection and relationship. It's very exciting to see them change and grow from day to day and to see the strides they're making.

Creating Rituals and Routines

Dusty's story beautifully captures why ritual and routine are so critical to modern family life. As Amy described, just knowing that from Friday evening until Saturday evening Dusty's presence is a certainty gives her the peace of mind to get through difficult times; it also gives their sons the consistency that children of all ages crave from their caregivers. His story also reveals that the rituals and routines that anchor and give balance to his family are both old and new; they are born from the need to create order in today's busy world and are also deeply rooted in his ethnic, cultural, religious, and personal history.

Dusty understands that the rituals of Judaism, such as observing Shabbat, are not just part of a cultural and religious tradition he values; they are the very threads that have kept families together and strong for generations, even through the darkest horrors of history. As a modern dad, Dusty has consciously woven his family life together with those same threads. This demonstrates not only a way of honoring his ancestors but also makes good sense; while finding balance in an increasingly scattered and fragmented culture is undoubtedly challenging, these rituals — having carried dads and families through much more difficult times in the past — are tried and true.

By reflecting or by talking with other family members, some dads may discover that, at least in part, the work of creating new rituals and routines has already been started. Just as Dusty had to arrive at a decision about actively incorporating the traditions, rituals, and routines of Judaism into his family life, another dad may learn about a powerful rite of passage for boys from a relative who follows the ethnic traditions of their family more closely. With some experience of attending Shabbat dinners at friends' homes, I found myself wondering if there was anything comparable in my Catholic background, and if not, how could we create a similar nonreligious, powerful ritual?

Not all of us may have much religious, ethnic, or personal history or tradition to draw on for our rituals and routines. Many of us may start anew, giving our children something they can pass on to their children. I recently worked with a small group of four dads who were using many of the activities in this book as the basis for a combination book club and dads' group. One of the dads, who happens to be a yoga teacher, described to the group how he came up with a ritual to share with his son regularly.

He and his boy were outside walking together, somewhere in nature, but not far from the city limits. As they talked, his son recounted their experience hiking in the mountains — Mt. Monadnock in New Hampshire, to be precise. A few days later, this dad noted that his boy mentioned the mountain experience yet again. At the next meeting of the dads' book club we discussed the

importance of creating a Ritual Dad Time with each of your children. In the following days, as this dad pondered what he could do
with his son for ritual dad time, he was suddenly struck with the
obvious answer: their ritual would be walking outdoors together in
different places in and around the city. Of course, when possible,
they would spend that ritual time hiking in the mountains.

MORE MODERN DADS: **Balance and Ritual for Road Dads**

Seth Miller, 42

FAMILY: married; father of three sons and one daughter
BORN IN: Boston, Massachusetts
LIVES IN: San Francisco, California
OCCUPATION: growth management consultant

Seth works about fifty hours per week as a senior program of-
ficer in the field of growth management and state policy for
the State of California and travels six to ten days per month.
His wife, Ruth, is a city attorney in San Francisco. Below you
will see how this father of four deals with traveling and family
life, as well as learn tips for Road Dads.

SETH: However many nights I'm away, it takes that many
nights to rebuild after the confusion or erosion of a routine
that happens while I'm gone. With twin boys, a toddler, and a
newborn, and both of us working full-time, our family operation
runs smoothly only when we stick to the schedule. Needless
to say, when I'm gone it's a lot for one person to manage.
Throw a sick kid into the mix (which always seems to happen
when I'm away) and you can imagine how well received I am
upon return.

We try to enlist help, but it's difficult to count on neighborhood babysitters, and in some cases too expensive. I have been fortunate enough to negotiate a work schedule that is flexible. It makes a huge difference. When I return from a trip, I try to pick up the boys right after school at 3:30 PM, do dinner and the nightly routine, and give Ruth time to do her thing. This helps mend the resentment that may have developed while I was traveling. It also allows me to bond with my boys and keep the hectic pace of work in perspective.

I find that pursuing utopia is counterproductive; the perfect balance between work and family at any one point is unattainable. One nightly ritual we have developed is something called "fire time." No matter who is home, away, or working late, we do it every night. It's very simple: we hold hands, light a candle, say a small prayer or sing a song, acknowledge who isn't there, and say something we did that day. Often it's short, but it adds consistency to our sometimes inconsistent lives. The kids remind us if we forget!

Tips for Road Dads

- *Frequent communication*: The more you stay in contact, by whatever means — texting, tweeting, calling, Skype, etc. — the more reassuring it is and the more connected you stay.
- *Fax a menu*: Share the details of your day — a menu, a doodle on your meeting notes, a map of the city you're in. Be creative; your kids can do the same.
- *Dad live*: Webcams are nothing short of a miracle. No matter if you're two thousand miles away, there you are live on camera. Skype or any number of others are great.

- *Leave your itinerary*: The more detailed the plan, the better. Your kids may even want to trace your journey on Google maps.
- *Go easy on gifts*: Bringing home too much loot too often leads to unrealistic expectations.
- *Ease in, ease out*: The traveling parent should adjust to the family's rhythm and routine, not the other way around.
- *Transitional objects*: With younger kids, give them something (a teddy bear, a doll, kisses on the hand) to remind them of you or to hold if and when they miss you.

Creating Ritual Dad Time

One great way to spend time with your child regularly is to create Ritual Dad Time. This is different from the daily rituals you may already do, like sharing meals, walking to school, and reading together. This is special, minimally once-a-month, one-on-one time with Dad. Think of it as the father-child equivalent of a couple's "date night." This ritual can be started at any time, with children of any age (newborn to adult). My daughter and I, for example, started a "daddy-daughter breakfast" when she was ten months old. Another dad I know and his teenage son alternate who decides on the activity each month. Dusty's ritual with his three boys, as you will see in the following pages, involves a parking garage and a special doughnut shop.

The purpose is to build in time for you and your child to foster your bond: to share stories, transmit your values, discuss important issues, or just enjoy each other's company in an unpressured way. Beyond whatever you do during Ritual Dad Time, the

true and lasting value comes from keeping your regular commitment to showing up for these special hours with your child. Here
are the steps.

Step One. Review these simple guidelines:

1. Get together as father and child at least once a month, for
    at least one to two hours and with only one child at a time
    (this may be difficult for larger families, but it's essential
    for building a one-on-one relationship).

    For live-away dads: Depending on how often you see
    your child, you could either do your ritual less frequently
    (every three, six, or twelve months) or do a long-distance
    ritual, such as a monthly letter or ongoing project.

2. Choose an activity you both agree on. You may allow your
    child to choose, or you can alternate who decides. I don't
    recommend making executive decisions, except in cases of
    extreme resistance (more on that below).

    Examples include: Going for a meal, taking a walk, vis-
    iting another town, going for a bike ride, cooking a meal
    from a foreign country, working on a building/fix-it proj-
    ect, taking a drive, going to a sporting event, playing a
    game, doing an art project.

    For dads with infants: Think about visiting a different
    environment to stimulate your child's senses, such as a park
    with a lot of birds, the beach, a crowded playground, or a
    quiet forest.

3. Make sure you talk during your time together. Going to a
    movie or a game is fine, as long as you talk at some point.
    Using what William Pollack (author of *Real Boys*) calls "ac-
    tion talk" (shooting baskets or playing video games while

talking) is great, but as men we also need to model face-to-
face dialogue for children of all ages. We don't always need
a distraction! Every three to four months, use your Ritual
Dad Time to do a Relationship Checkup (see chapter 6).

4. Be consistent. The ritual does not have to be on the same
    day each month, but make sure it happens so that your
    child can count on it. I suggest scheduling your next ritual
    time at the end of each time together.

Step Two. Make the pitch to your child (and expect resistance)

Express to your child that you would like to try this once a
month for six months. My suggestion is to make this your request,
something *you* are asking of *your child*. For example, a father I know
told his eleventh-grade daughter that he wanted to have time with
her before she went away to college; on the face of it, she would be
doing this for him. Also, make it clear that you have no other agenda
than to have fun and to spend time doing things your kids want to
do regularly.

If you are met with total resistance, I advocate making Dad
Ritual Time mandatory. That's right, mandatory. The resentment
and resistance will almost certainly fade. I once prescribed this
ritual time for a father and teenage son who were constantly in conflict with each other. Part of their problem was that they had too few
positive experiences together. Younger kids will be far less likely to
resist.

Finally, it's important to let your child's mother know up front
what you're doing. Doing so will reduce the likelihood of her feeling any resistance to the plan. Explain what you're doing and why
this ritual time is so important. Also, listen to and take her concerns
seriously. She may offer some good suggestions or tips as well.

Step Three. Keep a log of your Ritual Dad Time

Reflect on your experience each time by writing, even briefly, in a journal or on your computer. Think about what went well, things you discussed, what didn't go well, and so on. Plan on doing your ritual for at least six consecutive months.

If after the first or second month your ritual time is not going well, consider the following:

- Are you giving your child a choice about how the time is spent?
- Are you totally present during your time together (not talking on the cell phone, not stopping to run errands, not having the TV on)?
- Talk with your child's mother or a friend about what is happening, and ask for their suggestions.
- Talk with your child about ideas for what you could do to improve your time together.

Since you are initiating the ritual, you need to first look at your own behavior to see what you could change.

Dusty's log on the next page is a good example of some of the challenges involved with putting Ritual Dad Time into practice, as well as the moments of joy, laughter, and connection that come from sticking to your commitment. One of his log entries nicely captures the kind of meaningful conversation that can spontaneously happen during Ritual Dad Time. Similarly, the other entry shows the reality of how difficult it can be to do something as simple as taking his boys for doughnuts. These are poignant illustrations of what commitment and consistency really look like. The key to Ritual Dad Time is to remember that you will inevitably have that moment — just as Dusty did — when it feels like a fight to keep the ritual going. Too often, the easy

EXERCISE 8. Create Ritual Dad Time: DUSTY EBERS

I asked Dusty to describe his Ritual Dad Time and fill out the log below.

DESCRIBE YOUR RITUAL: *Most Sunday mornings we pile in the car (rain or shine) and first go for bagels and then hit the doughnut store. To be honest, it's more about the "getting" than the actual "eating." Although my boys love to eat! We have a very specific routine — we enter the parking garage from the same entrance each Sunday and we try our best to park in the same spot. We all cheer when we get the "good spot" because it is close to a short-cut right to the doughnut store.*

DATE: May 2, 2009

WHAT WE DID: *My two oldest boys and I went straight to the dough-nut shop!*

MY REFLECTIONS: *Today, in the car, Zak (my middle child) talked about birth order and when Grandpa became a daddy and when his daddy became a daddy and when he will become a daddy, etc. Also, along the same lines, we discussed work. They both talk about wanting to work with me when they grow up so we can have offices next to each other. I guess that's all they've known, since I've worked alongside my father for the last twelve years.*

NEXT RITUAL TIME (WHAT/WHEN): *Sunday, May 16, doughnuts!*

DATE: May 16, 2009

WHAT WE DID: *Doughnut shop with the boys*

MY REFLECTIONS: *Sometimes I have to fight really hard to keep this ritual going. Today nobody was in the mood, and I was tired, they were tired. But I have to be consistent. I know how important it is. This morning I had to remind myself that there wasn't any real obstacle in the way of us going and I know that when it's over, I'll be happy we stuck to it. We all thrive on ritual.*

NEXT RITUAL TIME (WHAT/WHEN): *Sunday, May 23, doughnuts!*

thing to do is justify putting it off or not make time in the first place. So, when that moment comes, try to keep in mind what Dusty did; children thrive on ritual. It's not *what* you do — it's that you *do* it.

Modern fatherhood offers us a new and potentially transformative identity as men. What if we viewed success less in terms of *what* we do and have and more in terms of *who* and how we are? What if manhood was measured, as it so often is, not by the size of our paycheck, the type of clothes we wear, the zip code we live in, or the kind of car we drive but by the quality of our relationships in our homes, at our workplace, and in our community? How would our priorities shift? What kind of impact would that kind of shift have on our physical and mental health? How would our loved ones, particularly the generations of children to come, be influenced by a masculinity that was defined less by work and more by relationships?

Living more balanced lives, weaving rituals and routines into our family relationships, and closing the gaps between what we *say* is important and how we actually spend our precious minutes, hours, and days are essential to developing lasting intimacy. In fact, intimacy with our children and loved ones is nearly impossible when the scales are tipped and we are unbalanced. Balance is a practice, not a destination.

CHAPTER 5

Know Your Children

How well do you really know your children? Would you consider yourself an expert on their lives? During my lectures I often give parents a pop quiz to illustrate why it's so important for us to ask ourselves these seemingly basic questions. The quiz addresses two main areas: what you know about your children's *outer life* — what they do, where they go, who they spend time with, how they behave — and what you know about your children's *inner life* — what they like and dislike, how they feel about themselves, what they hope for and worry about, who and what is important to them.

Given that children are perpetually changing, the quiz is meant to be done regularly. So, to get you started, why don't you take a mini-quiz and answer the following three questions drawn from the original, much longer quiz (see the full quiz on pages 116–17): *1. What recent accomplishment, big or small, is your child most proud of? 2. Name one of your child's big disappointments this year? 3. What are your child's current prized possessions?*

How did you do? To be absolutely sure, you would have to check with the source (or check with someone close to your child). While it feels really good to ace the quiz and equally awful to flunk, this exercise is not intended to qualify you for Dad of the Year; depending on many variables, such as when you take the quiz or how often you see your children, your results will undoubtedly vary. Not surprisingly, when I'm traveling heavily for lectures or approaching a big writing deadline, I often do poorly on questions about the daily happenings in my kids' lives; during such times, the quiz can truly serve as a wake-up call. Some of you may consistently do very well, in which case you can think of the quiz as affirming your expert status. Whether you are left feeling great or guilt ridden, quizzing yourself is meant to become second nature, a mental checklist of important things to know about your child that you run through regularly.

Below is the quiz completed by LeWayne Jones, whom you met in chapter 3 (p. 68) and we'll see again later in this chapter.

EXERCISE 9. Take the Modern Dad's Quiz: How Well Do You Know Your Children? LEWAYNE JONES

Take the following quiz alone. Answer all the questions you can for each of your children. When you finish, check your answers by talking directly with your child, your child's mother, or your partner. Make sure you fill in any questions you got wrong or left blank.

1. What recent accomplishment is your child most proud of? *She recently apologized to me, which took courage.*
2. Name one of your child's big disappointments this year. *She got a bad grade.*
3. What are your child's current prized possessions? *Her cell phone.*
4. What is your child's favorite food? *Shrimp.*

5. Can you name your child's teachers? *I can name three: Mr. Chilton, Mr. Burton, and Mrs. McCoy.*
6. Name two things your child did at school in the past two weeks. *She had a track meet and a big science project.*
7. What is most challenging about school for your child? *Staying on top of her grades.*
8. What does your child like about school? *Social life.*
9. What does your child like to do in his/her spare time? *She talks on the phone.*
10. What types of music does your child listen to? *R&B.*
11. Which TV shows, movies, actors/characters, and athletes are popular with your child and his/her friends? *Candace Parker and Kobe Bryant.*
12. What are his/her three favorite websites? *MySpace, YouTube, Disney.*
13. Does your child belong to any social networking websites (MySpace, Facebook, Club Penguin, etc.)? *Yes.*
14. What causes your child the greatest stress? *Peer pressure.*
15. Who are your child's close friends, and why does he/she like them? *Haley and Gabby.*
16. Who are your child's heroes and role models? *Her mom.*
17. What would your child like to be when he/she grows up? *A lawyer.*
18. What is something that really upsets your child? *When I don't give her all my attention.*
19. What does your child like to do with you? *Go to the movies and the mall.*
20. What does your child love about you? *My sense of humor.*

As you can see, LeWayne was, on this particular occasion when he took the quiz, very tuned into his daughter's life. When he doublechecked his answers with his daughter, he discovered he needed

only minor corrections. Knowing is a practice and a mindset. The quiz
is a tool for staying aware and tuned in over time.

Becoming an Expert on Your Children — Their Whole Lives

Every child craves the interest, attention, and presence of their primary caregivers. They need us to *know* who they are as unique individuals, not as vessels for our own grand plans or unrealized
dreams. The job of any parent is to be an expert about his child's life
— what scares her or brings her joy, what a certain look on his face
means, what she's doing in school, who his doctor is, who her
friends are. Just like any expert — a technology guru, a professional
athlete, a mechanic — as an expert on your kids you must to stay
current with the latest changes in your child's life.

Claiming expert status is a stretch for some dads, myself included. By being an expert on my daughter's life, for instance, I
communicate a clear, powerful message that she is worthy of time, interest, and attention to detail. The feeling of being valued and loved
simply for being herself builds the foundation for healthy self-esteem.
Older children as well as teens also need parents who genuinely take
an interest in their lives without the parents being overly intrusive.
Our kids want us in the background, on call, or standing by. Unfortunately, teens often have strange ways of asking their parents to be
there. For example, I often communicated my desire to be known by
my father or stepfather by getting into trouble.

If our sons and daughters don't feel that we know them,
chances are they won't tell us this. Both girls and boys often say their
silence is rooted in fear or resentment. Ironically, many are afraid to
tell their dad how rejected they feel, believing such honesty will only
upset their dad more and drive him farther away. Some fear their
dad will hear their words as criticism and get upset. Other young

people resent their dad's absence or disinterest and retaliate by quietly pulling back, leading their dad to believe the relationship is just fine. But the hurt and rejection can last a long, long time. Usually, if the child doesn't act out her feelings on others, she turns them inward. A young child may seek a dad's attention by becoming more defiant. A middle-schooler may develop an eating disorder or lose interest in academics. A teenager may experiment with drugs and alcohol. A child at any age may quietly give up trying, thinking she is not worthy of her dad's attention and interest.

When they are young, children use their parents as mirrors. Initially our behavior, emotional expressions, and responses influence our infant's developing sense of trust. As our babies become more autonomous, our mirroring grows increasingly important. If my four-year-old, Jake, shouts "No," and my response is to shout back, my anger gets reflected back to him and becomes internalized as fear or more anger. Gradually, as children learn reasoning and reflection and become more independent, they need us to mirror the limits of their behavior as well as interest and presence in their expanding world. When they reach school age, their sense of self becomes stronger, but they continue to absorb the feelings mirrored in our validation/disapproval, our encouragement/disinterest, and our consistency/unreliability. For example, a daughter whose dad mirrors appreciation for her quirky sense of humor is likely to take it in and think, "I must be funny and a good person to be with." By contrast, if she looks in the mirror to find a dad who makes empty promises and is always busy, she may think, "I must not be that interesting" or "Maybe I'm really not good enough for him." Remember, with school-age children, *everything* is personal.

While early adolescence is marked by an abrupt shift in priorities and values — and apparent disposal of the need for any mirroring — dads should not be deterred. Naturally, as children enter adolescence they want more independence. The five-year-old

daughter who wanted Dad to know her dolls' names by heart becomes the ten-year-old daughter who places Dad on a need-to-know
basis for just about everything. Even if our kids resist, push us away,
or shut us out, that does *not* mean we don't matter anymore. A father will always matter to his children. Even if we want to give them
more space and privacy, that does not mean we have to stop being
available and interested in what is happening in their lives.

Studies done with teens show they really do want parents involved in their lives. In her study of fathers and sons, researcher
Ricky Pelach-Galil found that when boys are around thirteen to
fourteen, the father becomes a central figure in their lives.[1] The boys
interviewed for the study reported paying close attention to their father's habits, values, and routines, as well as his interest in their lives.
This is, of course, the same age when boys are pushing away from
their parents to be with their friends.

Daughters are no different. In a large survey of girls in grades
eight to twelve, daughters consistently said they wanted more time
with their fathers, better communication, and a sense that their fathers were interested in their lives.[2] As one girl put it, "I wish my
father would try to understand me more."

Knowing our children is not only important to their health and
well-being but also a powerful form of risk prevention. One study
found that parental knowledge — being aware of your child's daily
activities, whereabouts, and companions — reduces the incidence
of teen drug use.[3] Parental knowledge is not simply about keeping
tabs or the occasional interrogation; it requires two-way communication. If an eighth-grade boy wants to give his dad the slip after
school or withhold information about his new friends, chances are
he could pull it off. If that same boy feels trusted, valued, and understood — that his parents *know* him — he won't need or even
want to keep them in the dark.

The following stories illustrate how you can develop this concept of knowing your child into a daily practice. Specifically, they give real-life examples of each of the four key elements to knowing: being *aware*, being *accessible*, being *active*, and being *attentive* (listening).

Lorne Michaels, 63

FAMILY: married; father of a daughter, eight, and two sons, twelve and sixteen

BORN IN: Toronto, Canada

LIVES IN: New York, New York

OCCUPATION: creator/executive producer of *Saturday Night Live*, executive producer of *30 Rock*, and Emmy Award–winning television and movie producer

Miraculously, I managed to avoid doing a double take. As a lifelong *SNL* fan, I knew instantly that the man standing behind the small crowd of dads gathered around me postlecture was indeed Lorne Michaels. As I tried focusing on answering a question from one of the dads, I couldn't help but wonder if I'd made a fool of myself by doing an impression of Stuart Smalley (Al Franken's hilariously mockable therapist who affirms himself in the mirror, saying, "I'm good enough, I'm smart enough, and gosh darn it, people like me"). Of course, Lorne wasn't patiently waiting to speak with me about Stuart Smalley; he simply wanted to say hello and thank me for the talk. I was impressed that he attended a lecture at his children's school, as I imagine many people as recognizable as he is don't make a habit of attending such events. Not only did he show up, but he was also very gracious and as down-to-earth as they come.

Three years later, I was looking to interview some dads who were active in their children's education and Lorne immediately came to mind. On a whim I thought I'd try to reach him. My call was returned the same afternoon I began my search. The following day, an interview at 30 Rockefeller Plaza was confirmed.

As you will see, being involved at school is only one of many key ways Lorne stays tuned in and active in his children's lives. In the section that follows, he establishes a critical element of *knowing* our children: *Awareness* of the distinction between *who we want our children to be* — which I believe is a very natural tendency most dads experience — and *who our children are becoming.* Without this awareness, it's too easy to unwittingly push your own agenda on your children, and nearly impossible to truly know them.

Who Are Your Children Going to Become?

LORNE: I've noticed with my sixteen-year-old that the more he's learned to stand on his own, the fewer phone calls I get. This is somebody I used to speak to, before he went away to school, every night for an hour or two before he went to bed. I'm really happy that he's enjoying his life enough that I'm no longer the person he *has* to talk to.

I think my job as a father is to make my children strong enough to walk away, and that is heartbreaking. I do it professionally as well, making [the cast] good enough to leave. It's a very hard thing because who wouldn't want to keep them young, dependent, and vulnerable? The key thing for me is that my children are not going to be the proof of my worth to the world — I'm not going to live through them. I'm not hoping to be able to say, "My kid's the president." It's not about that. It's a cliché, but every parent says, "I just want them to be happy." To me, that means feeling useful, feeling busy, and having the emotional capacity to connect, to be there for another person. The joy of being a dad is watching my children turn into *who they're going to be.*

I think it's naive to think your kids are a young version of you. Sure, you see yourself in them or say, "I remember that expression or I remember being confused by that," but they're not you. And you won't really find out who they are until much, much later. If they're fearful of expressing themselves or if the expectations are too high, it's likely you won't find out who they are at all. They still have to have rules — because in their perfect world my kids would just watch television all the time — and they still have to get their work done. But I can't make them into something they're not. I can practice with them — and I've thrown my fair share of pop-ups and passes — but I can't make them into better athletes.

What I'm getting at is that if you're observant and if you know your children — their eccentricities, their uniqueness — you begin to see more clearly the kind of kids they are, who they are at their core. As a dad, my job is to help my children truly be who they are, and that's where putting in the hours becomes so important.

Be Aware of Seeing Your Child as a Mini-Me

We all want the best for our children. It's only natural to want to protect them from making the same mistakes we made or to spare them unnecessary pain and disappointment. Likewise, most parents want to provide their children with opportunities they didn't have or didn't fully realize. These well-intentioned and usually healthy parenting instincts, however, need to be kept in check every step of the way. We need to avoid the temptation to see our children as extensions of ourselves. They are not Mini-Me's. In his vision of raising two sons and a daughter to be unique, emotionally connected, and happy individuals, Lorne reminds us of this simple yet critical truth when he says that your kids are not a younger version of you.

The potential problem with seeing your child as an extension of you is that he or she can easily become more of an *object* than an individual. Under the guise of "wanting the best for him" or "making sure she has opportunities I never had," you may unwittingly lose sight of who your child is or what she wants *for herself*. In other words, your influence and "guidance" can begin to overshadow your child's individuality.

The most common example I see in my work with parents — and a frequent theme in popular media — is the dad who pushes his child so hard to achieve his version of success that he fails to see other important aspects of his child's emerging personality. Maybe this dad is trying to exorcise his own demons (for example, he too had an overbearing father) or live out his own unrealized dream. Or he may simply be out of touch with his children's reality (for example, he grew up in poverty but his kids live in relative affluence). Without self-awareness about our own motivations as parents, we risk losing the connection to our children.

Another common example of this unhealthy dynamic is the parent who wears his child's accomplishments like a badge, as if the child is a walking (or crawling) résumé: "Cecilia's going to Yale in the fall," "Louisa's on three teams this season, probably MVP on two." There is nothing wrong with being proud. However, parents have to be careful not to overidentify with their children. Just as it's unhealthy to base our self-esteem on the size of our paycheck or the success we're having at work, so too is it unhealthy to base our self-esteem on our children's successes or failures. In his interview, Lorne summed up this point nicely: "My children are not going to be the proof of my worth to the world."

The poet Kahlil Gibran reminds us that in our role as parents, the only person we can truly control or change is ourselves:

> *Your children are not your children.*
> *They are the sons and daughters of Life's longing for itself.*
> *They come through you but not from you,*
> *And though they are with you yet they belong not to you.*[4]

These are wise but difficult words to live by. When you become increasingly aware of the ways you foster your child's emerging individuality, as well as the ways you may be pushing your own agenda too hard, your sense of *knowing* will grow and develop.

You Are the Furniture Your Children Sit On

LORNE: Parenting was a ride I really wanted to go on. At this point in my life, I know what my priorities are. Also, I'm in that rare, privileged position of being in control of my hours. If I was at a phase of my career where I had to prove myself, leaving at three o'clock would be harder to do. I work mostly nights, so I can be there to pick up my kids at school and also be there for most games and events. Generally, my schedule allows me to work around things. There are a lot of things I can deal with on the phone, even if I'm at a school event, but I try not to.

At one of my son's games, my phone rang, and I noticed that he wasn't playing; he was just sitting there on the sidelines. So I took the call. Later that night he mentioned it to me, and I said, "But you weren't on the field. You weren't playing." But it didn't matter; it was his time. I really took that to heart.

When I was growing up, my dad wasn't around much during the week. I remember that we did things together on Saturdays and Sundays. But with my mother, when I got home from school she would most likely be in the kitchen. It wasn't so much that I needed interaction with her; I just liked the feeling that she was there in case I needed her. I think it's a difficult balance — and everyone has to find it for themselves — of being overprotective or claustrophobic as a parent and just being around.

I don't believe in this idea of quality time. When my kids were younger, I used to say that they want you to be the furniture — you're the thing they sit on while they watch Nickelodeon. They just want you around. Also, I think if you don't put in the hours when they're young, you're going to be putting them in later when they're in therapy.

With the level of communications now, with email and cell phones, you're connected in these new ways. It's easy to be fooled into thinking you really *are* connected, but there is nothing like physically being there, especially while your kids are younger and still don't have a choice. Later when they do have a choice, it won't matter how many games you were at or how much you were around; you're just not going to get invited as often. Even though I'm able to show up at school and spend time with my children, I still feel like I should be around more.

Be Accessible by Showing Up in Different Ways

To realize his vision of raising children who feel unconditionally loved, encouraged to be true to themselves, and empowered to lead meaningful, emotionally connected lives, Lorne has become very clear about the need to be *accessible*.

I use the term *accessible* rather than *present* simply because it implies a greater sense of connection. The word *present*, especially when used in the context of fathering, is often associated with showing up in the physical sense; being there in body is very important, but not enough to build the intimacy and connection we all want with our children. They need to be able to *access* their dad, or as defined in the dictionary, "to make contact with; be able to reach, approach, speak with."

Lorne's exchange with his son about using the cell phone during one of his games is a great example of the need to be accessible, not merely present; when the issue came up later that night, his son made it crystal clear that showing up to his game and talking on the phone — being inaccessible — was a disappointment to him, even if he was on the bench. The fact that his son felt comfortable enough to discuss this issue illustrates some important practicalities to being accessible; Lorne listened without getting defensive or dismissive and then respectfully took his son's words to heart by agreeing to limit his cell phone use at games to emergencies only. Showing this kind of respect for a child is the essence of what builds trust and fosters self-esteem.

Can't technology also help us be more accessible as dads? Certainly, there are games that Lorne wouldn't be able to attend if he could not use his phone at all. I've heard many stories about the ways dads have become more accessible because of technology — the live-away dad who does video chats regularly with his daughters or the dad and son who text each other updates at different points during the day. Unfortunately, I've heard far more stories of dads who cannot seem to help themselves, answering calls constantly and tapping out emails any chance they get. These are examples of the various ways we as dads can delude ourselves into thinking we are accessible to our children, when in reality we are not. The lights may be on, as the saying goes, but nobody's home.

It is very easy to delude yourself into thinking that your children don't notice or don't care when you are inaccessible. Yet younger children and infants are especially attuned to their dad's comings and goings.

One simple yet powerful way to practice being accessible daily came from a dad I met at the Hudson Montessori School in Ohio. He described how every day that he's home — his work involves an enormous amount of travel — he spends fifteen minutes of uninterrupted time with each child, during which he focuses on making eye contact. I've done this with my daughter and found that almost immediately I felt more engaged with her and had a feeling of calm, as if time had slowed down. The key is not only consistently making time but also making eye contact (live-away dads can practice by looking at a picture of their child while talking on the phone). Amazingly, all the noise in your head disappears when your child is the sole focus. Even doing this for five minutes makes a difference.

Be Active in Your Child's Life

Much as it can be difficult to face, an essential ingredient to knowing your child is *time*, both quantity and quality. For most families
today, however, time can seem all too scarce. This explains why the
phrase *quality time*, which was initially used in the 1970s, continues
to be so popular, especially among dads. The idea was that by doing
something "meaningful" or "of quality" with his child, Dad could
make up for all the time he wasn't around. It was a way for parents
to "have it all," to work hard and stay connected at home.

Whether it was well-intentioned, a convenient justification, or
a way to relieve guilt, as a practical solution for the overextended
modern parent, "quality time" is inadequate at best. Children can
almost always feel when Dad expects a "meaningful experience."
Whether or not this expectation is explicitly stated, children often
end up feeling burdened by the pressure, which can be exacerbated
if they see their dad infrequently. Planning something special to do
with a child is one thing, but to have a certain outcome in mind is
a setup for disappointment. Real life isn't nonstop fun, and it certainly doesn't always go as planned.

In the ongoing quest for quality time, it's easy for dads to over-
look the importance of just being together with their child, whether
they choose just to hang out, to clean or fix stuff at home, to play,
to run errands, or to take a walk. Sociologist Michael Kimmel says,
"It's quantity time — hard hours of thankless, unnoticed drudge
work — that creates the foundation of intimacy."[5]

The idea of "quality versus quantity" is far too compartmental-
ized, as if parenting is something else to put in the schedule. A friend
and colleague of mine, Vince Durnan, who is head of a school in
Nashville, refers to this as "appointment parenting." In contrast,
Lorne gives us a wonderful and useful metaphor when he says children "want you to be the furniture . . . they just want you around."

Both Lorne and LeWayne, like many dads today, have prioritized being highly involved in their children's lives at school. If we think about where children spend the majority of their time — in daycares and schools — any dad who truly wants to know his child should find a way to get involved in his school or early childhood setting. Even dads with newborns or infants can begin early by participating in discussions and decisions about present or future childcare arrangements. Both parents, whether or not they still live together, have a stake in the care and education of their children.

I asked LeWayne to do the exercise on the following page to reflect on the different ways he's become an active dad at school. This exercise is intended to help you explore the range of ways you could be involved and, more importantly, what your child's school may need from you and other dads. Generally, most of us could be *more* involved in our child's school experience. If you are already very involved, this will get you thinking about *how* you are or could be involved. For example, instead of attending conferences and sporting events, maybe you could attend a parent night or volunteer your skills in the classroom or behind the scenes. If you are absolutely doing a great job already, this exercise will serve to increase your knowledge about your child's school. Think of this as a fact-finding mission.

We know from research that when dads (resident and non-resident alike) are more involved in the school community beyond just attending sporting events — volunteering, attending class and school events, showing up for conferences, and getting involved in the parent association — children get better grades, go farther with their education, and enjoy school more.[6] The benefits, however, are not limited to children. Dads learn about their children's social and educational lives, connect with other parents, and feel

EXERCISE 10. **Explore Different Ways to Get Involved at School:** LEWAYNE JONES

In order to learn about the many ways dads can get involved at school, do all four of the actions in the chart below.

Talk with at least 3 other dads about what they do (or know about). These might be dads you already know or you may step out and meet some new ones.

TEACHERS

Meet or talk with your child's teacher or a school administrator about ways they've seen dads get more involved and what needs they have.

OTHER DADS **PTA MEETINGS**

Talk with your child's mother (if not possible, a mother you know) about dad involvement from the mom's perspective. Is it important? Would it be welcomed?

MOTHER

Attend a PTO/PA meeting at least once. Find out about activities and events in which you could participate. Pay attention to the number of dads present.

Ideas

TEACHERS

The teachers and administrators do a good job of providing opportunities for dads to get involved at school, such as the dad's dinner. Conferences are also conveniently scheduled.

PTA MEETINGS

I have been to a lot of events and functions at the school that were put on by the Parents' Association, but not to a formal meeting.

MOTHERS

My wife, Renea, has really helped me stay connected with my daughter. She encourages me to go to school events as much as possible.

OTHER DADS

I end up talking a lot with other dads when I'm waiting to pick up my daughter after school. We actually discuss parenting, what's going on with our kids and what's happening at school.

like useful, knowledgeable participants, not sidelined observers. And moms — including single, married, widowed, divorced, or those in same-sex relationships — gain access to a community of adult male role models for their children and, if they've been the one primarily taking care of childcare and schooling, they're likely to feel more balanced.

There may be times when dads are literally too busy to show up at school. But it really comes down to values and priorities. LeWayne works full time and does much of the housework and childcare, but he also gets involved at school. Lorne may have the privilege of controlling his hours and often working at night, but he has no shortage of demands on his time. Being involved at school is a decision that dads have to make — dads like the one I met in a school in Reno, Nevada, Jorge Rojas. Jorge works a landscaping job by day and a security job at night but chooses to spend his one day off volunteering at his son's school. Dads across the socioeconomic spectrum can always find reasons *not* to get involved at their children's school. LeWayne, Lorne, and Jorge all understand, however, what many involved working mothers, single moms or dads, and stay-at-home parents with young children (who often work as hard as, if not harder than, many in the paid labor force) have known for some time: school involvement is not only important to children's educational success but is another way to stay connected and present in their lives.

Perhaps one of the most significant influences on Lorne's parenting concerns his family life growing up. His own father passed away when he was only fourteen, and the influence of having grown up with his uncle as his central father figure — a man whom he said was enormously important to him and very active in his life — can certainly be seen in Lorne's commitment to his own children.

Similarly, his uncle's role as a mentor affected Lorne's views on both fatherhood and his professional life at *Saturday Night Live*, the iconic late-night show he created more than thirty years ago. As he said earlier, "I think my job as a father is to make my children strong enough to walk away, and that is heartbreaking. I do it professionally as well, making [the cast] good enough to leave." Additionally, Lorne was well established in his work life, married, and in his late forties when he first became a dad. All these influences — upbringing, age, marital status, personal and financial success — have in some way shaped his desire, decisions, and ability to truly know his children.

MORE MODERN DADS: **Parental Knowledge as Risk Prevention**

John Cerepak, 54
FAMILY: divorced; father of a daughter, twenty-one, and a son, eighteen
BORN IN: Youngstown, Ohio
LIVES IN: Youngstown, Ohio
OCCUPATION: manufacturing supervisor

John is the father of an eighteen-year-old son and a twenty-one year-old daughter. He and their mother, Debbie, divorced when the children were six and four. When going through his divorce,

John committed to making sure that he and Debbie always communicated about the children. Their parenting wouldn't be seamless, but he wanted to make sure that his son and daughter knew that wherever they did their homework, ate their dinner, or slept, the rules and expectations would be the same. Not only that, but if something happened (that made them happy, that upset them) while they were at their mom's house, he wanted to know about it.

JOHN: Divorce isn't easy and isn't something you would wish on a family. It is — and was — devastating. And I can see how it can wreck a family forever, scar the parents and children. I didn't want to leave my children with that legacy. I wanted to do whatever I could to make sure I was and always would be an important part of their lives.

DEBBIE: It is a painful, painful thing to go through a divorce and to realize that you have to come up with a new vision for your life, for your future, without this other person. And when you are a parent, there are these other, incredibly vulnerable but important people to consider: your children. John and I are lucky in that we did not have an acrimonious divorce. It allowed us to focus beyond ourselves and our own needs.

JOHN: Deb and I are very fortunate that we have been able to maintain a friendly, cordial relationship. We put the children first. It is sometimes hard to do that even when you are married! You have work, all the stresses of daily life, and it can even be hard to know what is going on with your children when you are all under the same roof. But when there are two households, there is a lot of opportunity to miss things, both big and small.

DEBBIE: John and I live near each other — we're practically neighbors. We do not have to worry about the logistics of shuttling the kids around. This has helped keep their lives as "normal" as we could have hoped. The details of their daily life are the things we try to remember to pass along to each other: "Carly had a stressful day at school, Casey has a concert coming up, or one of them is in a terrible mood." Things that you might take for granted knowing within a family.

JOHN: When the kids are with Deb, I still feel very connected to them. We don't have to sort of start over each time they are with me. We don't have to catch up on a week's worth of events. I can ask them about things before they've even had a chance to mention them. Now that they are teenagers, it seems even harder to know what they are doing and thinking. If Deb and I didn't communicate, we could be missing a lot of important things or signals that our children might be making unhealthy choices. Between the two of us, we are sort of like detectives. We try to catch most things — in a good way.

DEBBIE: John is a very engaged father. Many dads I know have a hard time relating to their teenagers. But I think that because he made such a proactive decision to be there with them when they were still in middle school, he knows how to connect to them now. He made that big effort when they were younger, and that has paid off now that they don't need him — or don't think they need him — as much anymore. He has that foundation. They know he's there and watching and listening.

When I spoke with John and Debbie's two children, Casey and Carly, they described their parents' relationship as being much healthier than even many of their friends' parents' marriages.

Casey, eighteen years old, said that if he tells his mother something about his day, he is certain to hear about it five minutes
later at his dad's house.

John and Debbie have what's often called "parental knowledge"; they know the whereabouts of Casey and Carly, they
know their friends, what kinds of things they like to do. Parental
knowledge is an important factor in preventing drug and alcohol abuse, smoking, depression, and so on.

Unless You Listen, You Cannot Truly *Know* Your Child

LeWayne's upbringing was by many standards very traditional.
His dad was the provider, the head of the household, and, when
it came to discipline, the heavy. His mom did the majority of
the housework and child-rearing while also maintaining a career
in nursing. LeWayne felt known by his mother. She, like many
moms today and in generations past, was attuned to her children.
She didn't allow her nursing career to interfere with the more important work of raising her children. His father, while loving his
son no less, was not quite as interested in hearing about the emotional difficulty or confusion little LeWayne was experiencing as a
young boy.

As a result, most fathers like LeWayne's probably wouldn't do
very well on my quiz. In fact, most wouldn't even see the point of
it. This is not meant as a criticism; the "job" of most fathers,
LeWayne's included, was to bring home the bacon, not to find out
what his children were feeling.

LeWayne understands and celebrates the many gifts his father
gave him — his constant presence, the clarity he gave him about

right and wrong, a sense of security, a commitment to youth
sports, a model of a loving husband, a solid work ethic. Like many
dads today, LeWayne wants to continue his father's legacy in some
ways, and he wants to be a different kind of dad as well. LeWayne
wants to ace my quiz. He wants his children to have a voice. He
wants them to be assured that their thoughts and feelings really
matter to him.

LeWayne, however, understands something that many dads
don't always recognize: first and foremost, he needs to become a
more skilled and attentive listener.

Listen, Don't Fix

LEWAYNE: One of the biggest things I'm trying to do right now is
listen to my kids and understand what they're going through. When
they're talking to me and I find myself thinking, "That's not a big
deal," my mind steps in and says, "LeWayne, this is a big deal...
don't say another word!" Just listening makes such a difference.
Even when they say things like, "You don't understand, things are
different today," a lot of times they just want to be heard. It's not always easy, especially when they bring up tough issues. I want to attack it, give them answers, tell them I've been through it or that I
know best. I want to fix it. Instead, I try asking more questions, like,
"Why do you think she said that?" or "What was that like?"

I have a friend with two kids in college and one in high school.
He's a lawyer, so he's all about fixing problems. I've learned a lot
from him, but mostly by doing the opposite of what he does. Man,
there isn't a problem in the world this guy can't fix. He knows it all.
He's very, very controlling. I see how his kids react to that; they're
very smart intellectually, but they don't talk. They just do what
they're told and never step out of the box. And he'll tell you, "I've
seen it all. I've seen it all." That's his phrase. He probably has seen
a lot, but I think his kids need to see some of it for themselves!

With my son it's hard because I definitely go back to how I was raised by my dad, who used to say, "You're a man. You gotta suck it up." I still struggle with that a lot when my son goes through emotional issues. I preach to him, "Don't let 'em see your weakness, you gotta be strong in all situations." You do have to be strong, I mean, my dad was right in some ways, but that can just go too far. I really think I'm more in touch with my girls' emotional needs than I am with my boy's. There's something between me and him, and he knows it.

Last Father's Day, the kids gave me a card. My son, who's never written anything to me, wrote on the card: "I hope we can become better friends. We do a lot of things together but I just hope that we become better friends and I can really talk to you more about my life." That really hurt me because I thought I was doing things differently than my dad did, that my son felt closer to me. I thought I was doing pretty well on that one, but evidently I wasn't. I need to stop going on the attack when he brings up an emotional issue.

Don't Just Do Something, Sit There!

LeWayne has worked hard to be more attentive to his daughter, and it appears to be paying off. The habits he has developed when it comes to responding (or not responding) to his daughter are important to highlight: first, when his daughter says something that LeWayne wants to fix or react to, he is able to catch himself — on a good day, that is — before the words escape. He does two very skilled moves in the blink of an eye. First, he *recognizes* the urge to speak and tells himself that what his daughter has to say is important. Then, in the same split second, he actually achieves the Herculean task of *stopping himself* from saying anything.

This frees him up to actually listen to his daughter. Instead of there being two speakers and no listeners, there is one of each. Instead of shutting her down, he respectfully allows for some space to open up. Again, this is on a good day, but even if LeWayne gets the first part down — staying aware of his urge to respond, get defensive, be dismissive, and so forth — it will make a huge difference in his relationships.

LeWayne recognizes that if he wants his children to be open and to trust him, he can't try to fix or correct or advise or teach a lesson every time they share something. This is a great example of the day-to-day, moment-to-moment awareness required to build a different kind of father-child relationship. LeWayne is trying to walk his talk and not simply make proclamations such as, "I'm going to be different from my dad" or "I'll just do the opposite," which often end up being more bark than bite. He recognizes that a strong emotional connection with his kids isn't going to just happen on its own. It takes work and making mistakes.

Learning to be a better listener to his son presents LeWayne with some unique challenges. While he said he was surprised by what his son wrote on the Father's Day card, LeWayne also realizes that he's much harder on him than he is on his daughters. LeWayne recognizes in himself a strong resistance to his son's request for more connection. Like so many men, he seems ambivalent when it comes to such intimate matters of the heart; on the one hand he wants closeness with his son, which is why the Father's Day card struck a deep chord of sadness and pain. On the other hand, when given the opportunity to forge such a bond — when his son, for example, comes to him with an "emotional issue" — LeWayne often reacts by wanting him to "suck it up" and be tough. In *The Will to Change* bell hooks explains that part of what lies beneath this very common dynamic is the difficulty that we as adult men and women have in facing boys' pain. It's far easier, she says, to face or deal with boys' anger.[7]

By telling his son to suck it up, LeWayne perpetuates the all-too-common myth that he and millions of us were taught as boys:

showing your vulnerability is a sign of weakness. In my many discussions with boys about fathers, the overwhelming sentiment I hear from them is that dads are the ones who should take the initiative to address emotional issues in the relationship. LeWayne's son writing directly about his emotional needs was an act of courage as well as a tremendous gift that any dad would be lucky to get for Father's Day.

Despite his intellectual understanding of how this myth about manhood is damaging his relationship with his son, the challenge for LeWayne — and for so many other dads — is to change his behavior and truly be attentive to his needs. As he described in chapter 3, LeWayne believes that his biological limitations, combined with his upbringing, have left him largely ill equipped to attend to his children's emotions. Yet LeWayne uses neither the nature nor the nurture argument to excuse himself from what few men will readily admit to: LeWayne knows he needs to change and grow. Instead of fixing a problem — which in many cases means making it go away — the more difficult and more courageous thing to do is simply to bear witness.

There is no better way to shut down a child than to try and fix her problem, offer unsolicited advice, or, the root of all parenting evils, turn what she's saying into a lecture or a teachable moment. With a highly verbal six-year-old daughter and a four-year-old son who has yet to understand the concept of "one speaker at a time," I myself have no shortage of opportunities to walk my talk.

Listening, of course, is an imperfect art. My friend and colleague Terry Real taught that when listening to someone — it could be anyone — remember to put yourself *in the service* of the person speaking. That means putting your own issues aside, focusing fully on the other person, and doing everything you can to resist interrupting, getting defensive, correcting, denying, or behaving in any other way that turns the attention back on you. To have a constructive dialogue, there can only be one speaker and one listener at a time. Putting yourself in the service of your child and fully listening is truly a gift you can give anytime.

I gave LeWayne the following exercise to complete with his daughter. I originally designed it as a way for dads in my Dialogues with Dad workshops to get a reality check about how well their children think they listen. In the workshops, I first ask the children to rate their dad by assigning a percentage to each of the four kinds of

---

EXERCISE 11. Identify Your Listening Style: LEWAYNE JONES

Along with your child, review the following descriptions of the four kinds of listeners and ask your child to assign a percentage indicating how often you become each type of listener with him or her; at the same time rate yourself. Finally, compare your responses. Optional: Do the same exercise with your wife/partner or friend.

The Journalist

If there is one kind of listener who would be a good default, it's the Journalist. The Journalist asks good questions, some open-ended ("How are things with your friends?"), others closed ("Did you have a good time?"). Her body language lets the speaker know she is tuned in. She makes eye contact and nods, and her facial expressions reflect the speaker's words. She clarifies what the speaker says with an occasional "Is that right?" She also listens for what's not being said. The result is that the speaker feels very attended to, taken care of, and focused on. Young children, especially, need you to be the Journalist.

LeWayne: I am a Journalist <u>10</u> percent of the time.
My dad is a Journalist <u>0</u> percent of the time.

The Storyteller

The Storyteller relates to what the other person is saying by sharing similar stories. Sharing experiences can be a great way to show empathy, that you really "get it." However, if you start telling stories as the listener, it's easy for the speaker to feel that you're more interested in yourself than you are in him.

LeWayne: I am a Storyteller 30 percent of the time.
My dad is a Storyteller 40 percent of the time.

The Vacationer

The Vacationer is not really present for the speaker. Though he may appear to be listening, he is actually vacationing in his mind — thinking about work, somewhere he'd rather be, or the score of the ball game. This kind of listening can be great if the speaker simply wants to spew words or just talk at someone (who could be anyone). However, most people don't like talking to someone who is not really there. Usually, a speaker can tell when she is talking to a Vacationer.

LeWayne: I am a Vacationer 10 percent of the time.
My dad is a Vacationer 0 percent of the time.

The Handyman

This is the kind of listener, stereotypically speaking, that guys tend to like. The Handyman is useful. He's ready to fix any problem. He nods and listens intently, mainly with an ear toward what he can offer. The advantage of the Handyman is that sometimes people want to hear solutions. On the downside, sometimes people just want to be heard, not fixed.

LeWayne: I am a Handyman 50 percent of the time.
My dad is a Handyman 60 percent of the time.

listeners (they should add up to 100 percent total). At the same time, I ask the dads to rate themselves. Then the two come together, the dads try to guess what their child wrote, and they compare responses. Often I've found that dads are harder on themselves than their children are. As you can see from their assessments, LeWayne and his daughter are mostly in agreement about the kind of listener he is. Agreement is good but not the point of the exercise; for LeWayne, the takeaway is pretty clear: fix less, tell fewer stories, and learn to be more of a Journalist.

Here are some additional tips about becoming a skilled listener with your children:

1. *Listen for main ideas and feelings.* Pay attention to the important points your child is trying to make. What does she want you to "get"? Also, be aware of and acknowledge the emotions your child expresses. Similarly, if you think she is withholding emotions, simply mention it. For younger children this is especially critical; they need their parents to label and validate their feelings.

2. *As the listener, don't become the speaker.* As a listener, it's always tempting to relate your own story, give your opinion, or offer a solution. As a general rule, allow for breathing space or even silence before responding. There is nothing more frustrating than when the listener becomes the speaker. It is especially important to resist using what your child says as a springboard for teaching a lesson.

3. *If unsure about what the speaker needs from you, ask!* Sometimes a speaker wants to be listened to in a specific way; she may want you to give some advice, share your experience, or just be a sounding board and say nothing. If you're

uncertain what's needed, simply ask, "How can I be most helpful? Should I offer solutions, not say anything and just nod, share similar experiences?"

4. *Don't agree to be a listener if the time is not right.* Don't try to listen if you know you can't be present. Let's say you've just come home from work and your child (or partner) wants to talk. You start listening, but really you just want to relax for a few minutes first. Instead of just "yes-ing" them, be direct and tell them when you'll be more available to listen. Setting this kind of boundary is helpful to children of all ages. "I want to hear all about it! If you can give me five minutes to kick off my shoes, I'll be all ears. Sound good?"

Absence of Conflict Does Not Equal Closeness

I recently led a weekend retreat for dads and sons that was designed to help them strengthen their bond. According to the evaluations — which were filled out on Friday and then again on Sunday — I had done just the opposite; a majority of the dads actually reported feeling closer and more connected to their sons at the *beginning* of the weekend than at the end. I felt awful, and a bit confused.

Several days later, the director of the organization who hired me, Joe Caronna, called to say he had reviewed the evaluations and reached a very different conclusion. Before telling me, he described how his own experience with his son, Alex, at the retreat led to the new insight.

It began when Joe and Alex, fourteen, were doing the Relationship Checkup (detailed in chapter 6), which required each to respond to questions about their relationship. Joe asked Alex what he could do to improve their relationship, to be a better dad. Alex responded by saying he wished they spent more time together. Surprised, Joe's initial reaction was to get defensive and start justifying and explaining. Almost as if he had expected it, Alex calmly said he understood "all that provider stuff" and revised his request: "In the time that you don't have to work, can we get together more?" Joe's response matched the sophistication of Alex's question: Joe was elated that his fourteen-year-old was asking to spend more time with him and also feeling guilt-ridden that his son had to *ask* in the first place.

The two proceeded to chart exactly how much time in the past week Joe was not at work, and then how much of that nonwork time was spent with Alex. They quickly discovered, much to Joe's shock, how few minutes — not hours — they spent together as father and son. Joe was confused. As their conversation continued, it became clear that to Joe *any* time spent with his family qualified as bonding, whether they were all eating a meal, taking a drive, or just hanging around the house. Joe had no idea that from Alex's perspective, being in the same room but doing different things (i.e., Joe reading the paper while Alex played a video game) was not father-son bonding. Taking Alex's desire for one-on-one time to heart, Joe agreed to make the necessary changes. But something was still bothering Joe: How had he been so blind to Alex's needs, spent so little time with his son? Why did this all come as such a shock?

Days after the retreat, it hit him. Joe had convinced himself that because they had no major conflicts and enjoyed each other's company, everything with Alex was just fine. Besides, Alex had never said anything to the contrary. Joe now understood how he'd deluded himself into thinking things with Alex were better than they actually were. Had Alex not courageously and lovingly confronted him with a very different picture, Joe might have gone on believing he was spending more than only minutes each week with his son.

This is what led Joe to go back and look at the evaluations from the father-son retreat with a fresh perspective. The conclusion he reached was that on Friday, when the dads completed the beginning evaluation, many of them assumed everything was just fine. The dads reported feeling very close to and connected with their sons. By Sunday, those same dads had discovered, like Joe, that they really didn't know their sons quite as well as they thought. Specifically, most of the dads had no idea how much their sons yearned for their time and attention. Joe had enough humility, sense, and skill to recognize that Alex wasn't criticizing him as a dad, so there was no need to be defensive — which likely would have resulted in Alex shutting down. Instead, he used the moment as an opportunity to validate his son's perspective and to grow with him rather than away from him.

CHAPTER 6

Be Known by Your Children

When I start talking about our emotional lives as dads — using words like *needs, intimacy, vulnerability,* and *closeness* — to an auditorium filled with dads, a slight tension always enters the room. It's what I call the *group hug moment*: the unspoken fear that all this talk about emotions and relationships will inevitably lead to my asking the whole group to join me in one big embrace. Yet when I ask that same group to describe the kind of relationship they want with their children, every dad in that auditorium will say without hesitation that, above all, he wants to feel emotionally close and connected with his children. While I find plenty of humor in the *group hug moment*, it captures the central paradox and challenge of modern fatherhood and manhood: these so-called feminine or touchy-feely qualities we were raised to mock, disown, and devalue in ourselves and other males — emotional expression, vulnerability, sensitivity — are the very qualities (along with courage, strength, and other qualities associated with masculinity) we most want and need to build and sustain healthy, emotionally connected relationships as dads, husbands/partners, and friends. As modern dads we can and must resolve this confusing contradiction and show our sons and daughters that emotional connection and intimacy are positive, vital aspects of any male's life.

The research is clear: a close, emotionally connected dad-child relationship is a form of risk prevention and source of health and happiness for both child and father. Renowned researcher John Gottman found that children with emotionally available dads do better in school, have better peer relationships, and relate better with teachers than children with more emotionally distant dads. Children with dads who are critical or dismissing of emotions are more likely to do poorly in school, fight more with friends, and suffer poor health.[1] The National Longitudinal Study of Adolescent Health found that the single most protective factor for reducing behavioral risks, such as drug and alcohol use, early sexual activity, smoking, and depression, is children's connectedness to their parents; fathers were noted as being of particular importance.[2]

Interestingly, a study by the U.S. National Institute of Mental Health found that fathers who were actively involved in their children's lives had fewer accidental deaths, fewer premature deaths, less substance abuse, and fewer hospital admissions.[3] Not only is a close father-child relationship good for children, but it's a positive aspect of men's physical and mental health. In the preceding chapter, the focus was on *knowing*, the need all children have for a dad who listens, pays attention, is accessible, and is an active presence in their lives. This chapter introduces the importance of also *being known* by our children using storytelling. To help you continue both *knowing* and *being known* over time, the chapter details how to use a powerful, practical tool, the Relationship Checkup.

The Power of Your Story

Being known means letting down the walls and sharing your story. It means having the courage to show your flaws, fears, and joys. This is not to say that one should overburden a child with inappropriate revelations; rather, it's about giving your child the gift of knowing who you are and what you feel on a regular basis.

As I mentioned in the introduction, when I visit schools and lead a student workshop, I ask kids to anonymously write down two questions they would like to ask their dad but never have. I collect the questions and periodically tally the responses to determine the most popular ones. They turn out to be: "What was your relationship like with your dad?" and "What were you like as a kid?" These and all the other questions children have for their fathers point to what I call the elephant in the living room of child development: the missing stories of men's lives, particularly men's emotional lives. A child wants and needs her father's stories so that she can better understand who she is and where she comes from. Stories are gifts that every child deserves.

Children want real stories about who you were (and are) as a person, not just as their dad. War stories can be fun, but here I'm talking about letting your kids into your experiences with winning and losing, being embarrassed and feeling anxious, overcoming challenges and giving up. But what stories are appropriate to share with a child? The short answer is, trust your gut. If your gut says telling a story about your father's drinking will be upsetting, don't tell it. If, however, you have a history of your gut getting you into trouble, then check it out with a trusted friend or partner. While there are no hard-and-fast rules for storytelling, here are a few guidelines:

- *Let your stories emerge naturally and in context; don't over-whelm your child with your entire life story on a Saturday afternoon.* Your daughter loses a game: "Did I ever tell you about what my dad used to do when I would lose?"

- *Don't just be a reactive storyteller; take the lead.* "When I was in fifth grade, I was really concerned about what other people thought of me. Do you ever feel that way?"
- *Share stories about your present, not just your past.* "Sometimes I have trouble keeping my mouth shut. I was in this meeting the other day..."
- *Include feelings in your stories, not just facts.* Children need to know that you get scared, worried, joyful, excited, and so on. By labeling your feelings, you help children understand their own.
- *Be mindful of how your stories may be used against you.* If you decide to tell your teenage son about past alcohol or drug use, I suggest you prepare a response in case he uses that story to justify his own use.
- *When telling stories about your father, keep in mind that your children have a relationship with their grandfather.* If your child has a more positive relationship with your dad than you did, do not divide your child's loyalties. Talk more about the things you are trying to do differently. If your father was abusive, seek professional advice before sharing such stories. Remind yourself that stories are the lifeblood connecting generations.

The following story shows how a single dad uses the power of storytelling to stay connected with his daughter. He mines his own childhood for everyday experiences that his daughter may be able to relate to. Not only do these stories humanize him in her eyes, but they are also an effective way to initiate conversations about what matters most to his daughter.

Jonah Matranga, 39

FAMILY: divorced; father of a daughter, Hannah, thirteen
BORN IN: Boston, Massachusetts
LIVES IN: San Francisco, California
OCCUPATION: professional musician

When I was twenty-five, my best friend called me up to say his former girlfriend was pregnant and he was going to be a dad. At the time, Jonah was living with his band mates and playing gigs on the road incessantly. I remember wondering how he was going to manage fatherhood. Knowing what I did about his past — his dad was loving, but self-destructive, alcoholic, and absent for the majority of Jonah's adult life — I worried, as did Jonah, that the legacy of absence would continue.

The great irony of Jonah as a dad is that despite being a successful career rock 'n' roller, his parenting style couldn't be further from the stereotype; it's actually much closer to what's thought of as traditional parenting in most respects. He is a firm disciplinarian, pays close attention to Hannah's media intake, and is very active in the parent organization at her school. All types aside, the bottom line is that Jonah and Hannah have a special bond that is built on a foundation of mutual respect, honest communication, and solid commitment; and like any father and child, they have struggles, celebrations, and everything in between. In the following pages you will see how this father and daughter build and continue developing their relationship.

As my best friend, Jonah agreed to participate in my first

documentary film, *All Men Are Sons: Exploring the Legacy of Fatherhood*. I periodically interviewed him and Hannah over a period of about four years. Additionally, Jonah and Hannah have been my test cases for the new exercises I developed for dads and kids. The following interviews and exercises refer to Hannah at nine years old. At the end of the chapter is an exercise completed by Hannah at thirteen. The result is a unique story of how this dad and daughter's relationship grows and changes over time.

"Trouble of the Day" Stories

JONAH: Hannah splits her time about 70/30 between her mom (Heather) and me. I have her every other Thursday through Monday. And when it's not regular, like when I'm on tour or something else is going on, then we just catch as catch can, but it almost always ends up being about ten days a month, one way or another. Her mom lives seven blocks away, so we're close geographically, and things are good personally too. Once in a while we'll have a dinner together, so it works out well.

I feel like Hannah and I have a really tight bond. A big part of it is just showing up. It sounds so simple, but being involved in her school has been huge. The fact that her friends know me is huge. The one thing that my weird musician life really helps with is that I'm different from a lot of other dads; I'm around a lot more. I also look and dress different. Her friends have seen me in videos and heard my music, so that gives me a sort of cachet.

All I've ever tried to do is speak to her like a grown-up. Even when she was really little, we never did baby talk. I try not to talk down to her. Obviously, I try to keep my conversations with her age appropriate and to give her clear explanations of things she might not understand. But ultimately, I try to give her the benefit of the doubt, and I think that goes a long way toward our connection.

I've always told her stories about my life. When she was really little we did "trouble of the day stories," where each day I'd tell her about some small trouble I got into when I was young. Luckily, I have a lot of these stories! The only thing was, obviously, keeping them PG. It started when she had her first experience getting into trouble. I told her about a time when I got into trouble, and she really liked that. It went on from there.

Once I told her about a time when I took money from my mom's wallet. Well, actually, I was looking for money in there, but she didn't have any cash, just checks. So I took a check and made it out to myself, with no understanding of how checks worked, of course. Two weeks later my mom asked me if I had taken ten dollars from her wallet. I said, "No." Then she showed me the check with my terrible chicken scratch signature on it. Amazingly, they actually had cashed the check! I was a little reticent to talk to Hannah about stealing the money because I didn't want to give her any wrong ideas.

Since Hannah is nine years old, I don't tell any stories about anything involving sex or drugs. The one time I ever got a little worried about her and boys, I asked her if any of her friends were doing stuff that she's uncomfortable with. It became pretty clear that she and her friends weren't getting into nearly as much trouble as I was getting into when I was a kid, so I laid off. I realized that I was probably just starting trouble more than I was helping her.

She's nine, so I try to tell stories from when I was that age. I tell her about lying. Dishonesty seems to be a theme at that age, trying to figure out what's right and wrong, what she can get away with. Essentially, most of it's pretty innocent.

Telling Meaningful and Relevant Stories

One reason Jonah was able to connect with Hannah through storytelling was that the stories he told were meaningful and relevant to his daughter. His involvement in the different facets of her life gives him plenty of context for and understanding of what stories will most interest her. He makes a point of being very tuned into Hannah's social life. Not only is this a sign that he respects his daughter — that he cares enough to make time to know her friends — but it's also a nonintrusive way of being a knowledgeable, engaged parent. Sharing stories from our own pasts, with little understanding of our children's daily lives at home, with friends, and in school, only increases the odds of missing the mark and telling your child stories that are irrelevant. It is important, however, to remember that you may find it difficult to tell stories about some subjects — sex, relationship violence, self-esteem — but that does not mean they are irrelevant or shouldn't be addressed in another way. Talking about or analyzing a movie, for example, that depicts teen dating violence with a daughter who is not yet dating can be a powerful form of prevention.

The exercise on the facing page will help prompt you into thinking of stories you can share with your child about your life. Think about which ones would be most relevant to your children. If you're not sure, you can either ask your children or simply spend more time paying attention to what's going on in their lives. In some cases, you may want to modify the prompt so that your story is age appropriate.

In Jonah's case he found a powerful theme — trouble — from his childhood and told more frequent stories. There are many different ways to use the prompts. Choose what works best for you.

In the next section you will meet a father and son who continue to work on deepening their relationship, even into the son's adulthood. This story captures the determination, vulnerability, and love that are required in breaking intergenerational cycles of disconnection. These two men serve as great reminders that intimacy and connection, knowing and being known, can be addressed at any age; each generation has the opportunity to heal the past and build bridges to the future.

EXERCISE 12. **Find the Right Stories:** JONAH MATRANGA

Each story topic (left column) has a writing prompt next to it. You may choose to write down some of your stories and keep them as a journal for your children. You could also write these stories as letters to your children to help them learn more about you. This is an especially good idea for those with young children. Finally, share at least one story about yourself when you were your child's current age each week until you've completed the list below. If doing this face-to-face is not possible, you may use phone, letters (handwritten or emailed), video (live or recorded), or other creative ways. Consider also using ritual time (see chapter 4) as a venue to share your stories.

STORY TOPIC	WRITING PROMPT
Family relationships	Dinner at my home growing up…
Friendships	When I was young, my friends…
Getting in trouble	I got in trouble for…
School	I was the kind of student who…
Work	The best/worst job I ever had…
Self-esteem	I felt good/bad about myself…
Body image/Puberty	When I looked in the mirror…
Making decisions	I knew it had to be done, but…
Peer pressure/Fitting in	I knew if I didn't…
Competition	My thrill of victory/agony of defeat…
Interests	Nothing excited me more than…
Attraction/Dating	My first crush…
Sex	Something I wish I knew about sex then…
Spirituality	I believe…
Being irresponsible	I can't believe I…
Money	I've learned that money…
Popular culture	I would do anything to listen/see…

William (Bill) Lawrence Burke III, 61

FAMILY: married; father of four sons, thirty-one,
twenty-eight, twenty-five, and twenty-two
BORN IN: Boston, Massachusetts
LIVES IN: Needham, Massachusetts
OCCUPATION: head of school, St. Sebastian's School

Allow Yourself to Be Known

In selecting the dads to interview for this book, I made sure to include my friend and mentor, Bill Burke. Bill is one of those rare people who, after you've spent just a short time with him, leaves you feeling like you're the most important person he'll see all year. Simply put, he is interested. He wants to know... you. Bill writes a personal, handwritten letter to each of the graduating seniors at the high school he leads. He makes it his job to communicate that he *knows* and cares for each of the boys in his school. As a father of four boys, Bill does the same for his own sons, only they each get poems on their birthday. He has been doing this for the past twenty years!

Having talked with Bill for hours at a time, I've come to learn more about his experience as a son and as a father. I have always wondered if Bill, someone who genuinely knows and generously attends to the needs of others, allowed himself to be known as well. As I began conceiving this book, and this chapter in particular, Bill's name came to mind immediately. He was gracious and courageous enough, as was his eldest son, William IV (Will), to open up and share their stories.

Sharing Your Struggles

BILL: In *A Choice of Heroes*, Mark Gerzon wrote that the world will forever be different now because fathers are present when their children are born.[4] My wife, through all the Lamaze classes and the twenty-two hours of painful labor of her first birth, kept telling me how important I was. And I just didn't feel it. I felt like I was the fifth manager on the football team. She had this life growing within her, and I was this very replaceable spare part. And then the child was born. It's a transformative, miraculous moment, and you would have to be a very cold, hard-hearted person not to be forever warmed by it. So I think Gerzon is on to something there.

My wife and I have four sons. When the first one, Will, was born on January 4, 1977, a year and a day after we were married, we were ready for him. We just couldn't wait to be parents, and that's been our focus, every step of the way. I write each of my sons a poem on his birthday. I've been doing it for almost twenty years. Two of our sons are married now. I was able to read those poems from when they were eight and ten and twelve and twenty-six at the rehearsal dinners and at the weddings. I do it to have a record of who the children were then in my eyes. I keep the letters that they write me, and it's been incredibly rewarding.

I remember Will writing to me once saying, "You're just such a loving father, you spent so much time with us, where did this come from? I know it wasn't modeled for you." What matters to you, you attend to, and what you attend to matters. I attend to my children. When I get Red Sox tickets, if my wife is working, I only ask my sons to go with me. I don't think of bringing a buddy. That's where I want to be, with my kids.

My wife is a psychologist. A few years ago she said, "Bill, in all these stories you tell your sons — and you tell a lot of them — you don't share any of your struggles with them. You don't really share your failures with them."

Patty always reminds me to show my vulnerabilities, to share with our kids the things that didn't go so well. I do want to change; I want to invite more real conversation from my kids.

William (Will) Lawrence Burke IV, 31

FAMILY: married; father of a son, three, and a daughter, five

BORN IN: Holderness, New Hampshire

LIVES IN: Los Angeles, California

OCCUPATION: staff writer for *Jimmy Kimmel Live!*

The Flawless Man

WILL: My dad loves being a dad. I've always known and felt that, and I don't think there's a greater gift that you can give a kid than telling them, "I love being a dad, I love being with you, I love playing with you." He was just always very hands-on. Anything I am as a father is a credit to my dad. He's a great father. I am trying to do some things differently than he would, but in the grand scheme, I think he's amazing. And he didn't have a great model.

My grandfather had my dad's whole life mapped out for him. He was going to be the starting goalie at either Colgate or Middlebury or a good school. He was going to get into law school, and he was going to clerk for a judge in New York City. He was going to become an attorney just like my grandfather. Then my dad didn't get into law school. I think he still has a lot of shame about that. That's why he went into teaching and coaching.

Years later, when my grandfather was near the end of his life, my dad was talking about maybe leaving teaching. My grandfather turned to my dad and said, "Are you kidding me? I'd kill for what you have — it's the perfect life, the perfect job." And until that point my dad had always thought he was a failure in his father's eyes. My grandfather, who was not a man who shared his emotions, finally said he was proud of him. And my dad never would have known that if he hadn't broached the subject with him. So my dad has gone the other way — he tells us he loves us all the time and is extremely effusive and very forthcoming with his emotions and his pride.

In a different way, though, he still is "Bill the second" because he's hiding, he isn't all there for us. When we were kids, he was a wild and crazy guy, he'd have a few beers and people would be over, and everyone called him "Burkie." And now he's Mr. Burke. So he became the headmaster to the St. Sebastian's family — and then we all went there — and now that's who he is to us. He's still wacky and gets silly with our kids, his grandkids, but he continues to have a hard time admitting that he's been imperfect in any way. He's created the mythology of Bill Burke, the great dad, the perfect guy, a wonderful headmaster, the flawless man.

Pulling Back the Curtain

A common thread runs through the stories above, through Jonah and Hannah's and Bill and Will's, and really, through all father-child relationships: handling vulnerability and imperfection. But while Jonah makes a point of highlighting his own imperfections when he was a boy — telling trouble stories — Bill struggles to share what he perceives as his own weaknesses or shortcomings with his adult son. Will, as a son, has great insight into his father's struggle with vulnerability and, as you will learn in more depth below, he is also very clear about not wanting to pass on this legacy of disconnection to his own son.

Of course, there are certain imperfections a dad might not want to share with his children, but by the time they reach kindergarten, most children have at least begun to question Dad-as-the-Great-Oz. If they haven't by then, it's not long before they pull the curtain back altogether.

By explicitly sharing some of his foibles with Hannah, Jonah is teaching her that even dads don't have it all together and that, in turn, her mistakes are also forgivable. Imperfection is central to the human condition. Yet so often as dads we want to pretend that is simply not the case and don't allow important parts of ourselves to be known.

There is much to be gained by allowing our children to see us grapple with imperfection. By showing them, for example, that we need help or support at times or that we can own up to mistakes, we actually can build trust with our children. Vulnerability and accountability are foundations of intimacy and connection. If, on the other hand, we attempt to propagate the myth of our own infallibility — for example, by belligerently insisting on always being right, mysteriously retreating behind a facade of indifference, or adeptly using humor to deflect any possibility that something or someone has bothered us — we ultimately foster uncertainty and mistrust in our relationship with our children.

Bill, Jonah, and Will (as a father) all share the common desire to build, strengthen, and deepen the emotional connection with their children; more important, they are willing to take action, even when it means stepping out of what is familiar and comfortable. In short, they are committed to what is an essential reframing of traditional masculinity and fatherhood: prioritizing their relationships, looking inside themselves, welcoming support from others, using available tools, skills, or resources, and valuing growth and change. In the following section, you will see an example of how Jonah and Hannah, and Bill and Will, use a practical tool, the Relationship Checkup, to open the lines of communication and create what is a life-changing dialogue between father and child.

MORE MODERN DADS: Staying Connected at a Distance

Ralph Covert, 41
FAMILY: father of a daughter, thirteen, and stepfather of
two daughters, nine and eleven
BORN IN: South Dakota
LIVES IN: Chicago
OCCUPATION: Grammy nominated musician, creator of
Ralph's World

He's been called the Elvis of children's music. His is the voice to which many of us dance around the living room with our young children. Ralph has brought so many parents and children together through his music, so I was interested in his experience as a dad. After meeting him at a show, I asked to interview him. Despite the pain of living two thousand miles from his teenage daughter (who lives with her mother in Los Angeles), I discovered that Ralph's creative approach to staying connected — knowing and being known — was as unique, positive, and educational as the messages that come through his music.

RALPH: My career keeps me two thousand miles from my daughter, and it is what I have to do. When I see her, I want to spend every moment together. But that isn't what dads and teenage daughters do. So I have to let go and try to accept that I'm not exactly the center of her universe.

There was a time when I tried to come up with all these great things to do: going shopping, eating out, taking trips together — things that would make her want to spend time with me. But I realized that if I didn't make an effort to connect with her in little ways, not just extravagant ones, we would just be going through the motions and I wouldn't really understand what was on her mind.

I try to balance the day-to-day events of life — asking her about her day, what is going on in school, about her friends, the music she likes, the movies she's seen — with the bigger picture, of really trying to understand who she is and what makes her tick. I want to know what makes her happy and what she thinks is funny. And it is hard to not be there for the small events of life that she shares with her mother.

I also want her to know who I am. To know what my values

are and to help, in some way, to guide her. I don't want to sound preachy, especially from a distance. So I try to do my best to lead my life as best I can when I'm with her and when I'm away, so that she will know what is important to me.

I think the thing I want her to know first and foremost is how important she is to me. I try to demonstrate that in ways that aren't materialistic. That is the easy stuff — buying things to make your child happy. I don't necessarily want her to know how hard it is for me to parent from a distance, and I don't want to become her "friend."

I used to do anything to avoid having a conflict with her when we were together. I just wanted it all to be perfect. But that isn't reality. And I want to be real with her. I feel as though it is more important for us to be ourselves and work through a conflict, and learn about each other through it, than to sugar-coat everything.

The Ongoing Heart-to-Heart: Using the Relationship Checkup

Having what I call an "ongoing heart-to-heart" is a great way to bring these two elements of emotional connection — knowing and being known — together. It is a practical way for you and your children (adult children included) to communicate consistently and honestly about daily happenings and, most important, about the quality of your relationship. It also provides you both with a built-in mechanism for handling difficult conversations, whether the subject is unresolved from the past, currently happening, or in the future.

Many of us associate the term *heart-to-heart* with a father as a necessarily dramatic, confrontational, or highly charged moment — often brought on by some crisis or unavoidable circumstance

— in which one or both people bare their souls. The ongoing heart-to-heart, while it may at times be intense, is intended to be very different. No drama. No release of pent-up emotions. No crisis. In fact, I believe we can largely do away with the frequently depicted scenes in movies (unfortunately, based on common experiences in reality) in which a father finally opens up to his adult children at the end of his life or in which adult children regret not taking or having the opportunity to speak honestly with their father.

Early on in my work with dads, I knew that to have an ongoing heart-to-heart with their children, dads needed a tangible, practical, and structured guide. What started as an idea with a few questions on a slide for dads to use at home, the ongoing heart-to-heart has been developed into a tool — which has become the basis of my Dialogues with Dad program — called the Modern Dad's Relationship Checkup. At its core, the Relationship Checkup is about normalizing truth-telling, speaking from one's heart, and listening deeply, for dads and children (adult children included) on a regular, lifelong basis.

Practically, the Relationship Checkup is a series of questions designed and sequenced to initiate and encourage ongoing dialogue between dads and children. It's a structured way to have a heart-to-heart talk about two central themes: your everyday lives and your relationship with each other. There are two versions of the Relationship Checkup. Version one is for children aged five to ten, and version two is for children aged eleven and above.

To illustrate how this powerful tool works, below are excerpts from Jonah and Hannah's and Bill and Will's Relationship Checkups, along with their brief reflections about the experience. Following these excerpts, I have outlined the key lessons we can learn from the Relationship Checkup, as well as points on how you can best apply this in your own dad-child relationship. To help them most effectively use this tool, I ask dad and child to follow a specific step-by-step process for introducing and doing the Relationship Checkup, which is given in greater detail in the appendix and summarized in the excerpts below.

EXERCISE 13. The Modern Dad's Relationship Checkup: Excerpts from Hannah (age nine) and Jonah

Jonah and Hannah first found a quiet place where they wouldn't be interrupted (his apartment), reviewed the list of questions together, separated and each wrote their individual responses to all the questions, and finally came back together and shared their responses to each question aloud.

Hannah's Responses

1. **Positive qualities I bring to our relationship are:** *That even though I don't get to see you as often as I see Mom, when I do get to I make sure we have fun and try not to get in arguments, which we hardly do.*
2. **Positive qualities you bring to our relationship are:** *That you know when to be serious and when to joke around and be funny.*
3. **Ways that I sometimes make our relationship difficult are:** *I sometimes disagree with you, even though I know you are saying the right thing. Sometimes I just do it to get my way, even though what you are saying is the better thing to do.*
4. **Ways that you sometimes make our relationship difficult are:** *I don't think you make anything difficult. It is just kind of hard to see you be all nice and funny and then turn into the firm dad.*
5. **One way I can strengthen our relationship is:** *To focus and listen more to what you're telling me, because it's usually important.*

6. One way that you can strengthen our relationship is: *To not be on the phone as much, even though you have gotten way better at that.*

7. One of my greatest fears is: *My family members dying or my family members going away and never coming back.*

8. I think one of your greatest fears is: *For me to turn out to be a bad person or to use drugs or alcohol. For me to dress inappropriately and have a bad personality.*

9. I think one of the best things you've done for me is: *In general just having patience and being willing to do things for me, even though you just really want to sit at our computer or sleep.*

10. I think one of the best things I have done for you is: *Trying to listen and not to forget things as much, although sometimes I do.*

11. If today were our last day together, one thing I would want to make sure you know is: *That I love you.*

Jonah's Responses

1. Positive qualities I bring to our relationship are: *That I am encouraging and supportive and that I maintain a good balance between having fun and being responsible. I'm not too boring but also not too crazy. I listen to you and try to let you make up your own mind.*

2. Positive qualities you bring to our relationship are: *You're honest with me and very caring. You listen to my advice, but you still think for yourself.*

3. Ways that I sometimes make our relationship difficult are: *Being scattered or in a hurry, not managing my time well, being on the cell phone and the computer too much. Being too firm sometimes when I just need to be patient or gentler.*

4. Ways that you sometimes make our relationship difficult are: *Asking for things too much when I've already given an answer. Not saying or asking for things directly (asking questions leading up to what you really want to ask).*

5. One way that I can strengthen our relationship is: *By being*

clearer about my schedule and managing my time better, so that when we're together, we can make the most of our time and have as much fun (and get as much done as we need to) as possible.

6. **One way that you can strengthen our relationship is:** By being more direct with me about your feelings and being more patient when you can't have what you want right away.

7. **One of my greatest fears is:** That I go away too much and that you'll be mad at me later on for that.

8. **I think one of your greatest fears is:** That I'll be mad at you if you make a mistake or don't do well in school.

9. **I think one of the best things you've done for me is:** Reminded me how precious life is and made sure I'm spending it doing things that make me feel alive, things that I really love. You've also reminded me over and over again to be kinder and more patient.

10. **I think one of the best things I have done for you is:** Given you a sense of self-respect and the knowledge that you're beautiful inside and out, and that it's okay to have fun and also to be serious and to really try hard. Also, that it's important to try to find what you love, what's really important to you (like being a father and making art is for me), and then to make your life be about that.

11. **If today were our last day together, one thing I would want to make sure you know is:** That I have tried as hard as I can to balance my dreams of being a great artist and my dreams of being a great father. Also, that we belong to each other. You taught me that.

Reflections on Doing the Relationship Checkup

JONAH: Hannah was resistant to doing the Relationship Checkup at first. You know, "What's the point of this? This feels weird, this is stupid": all the stuff you'd expect from a nine-year-old. I just said, "I know. Let's just do it and see how it feels. It will be over soon." I tried to present it as plainly as possible.

So she reluctantly agreed. I thought it was awesome, and afterward she said she really loved it too. It helped us put words to a lot of the things that I think are said in our actions. But to say them out loud was really helpful. We didn't have to have some big exhaustive discussion. I think just writing things down and seeing them on the page was great. I know things are sinking in, so I don't have to give a big "moral of the story" thing.

I was surprised by her answer to "one of the best things I've done for you." She said that she's really trying to listen and not to forget things as much. That was really great for me to hear, to know that she's aware of these things. For the best thing that I've done for her, she wrote "having patience and being willing to do things for me, even though you really want to sit at our computer or sleep." There's obviously some darkness in there because I know that she perceives me as someone who wants to either do work or to sleep, and that's not good. But on the lighter side, what it says to me is that she sees that I want to be there for her and that I can put her needs above mine. And that's great to know.

I imagine that she sees doing this kind of exercise as my trying to care for her and pay attention to her. I think that ultimately most parents can agree that all kids want is attention. You try to make it positive and constructive. If you can get a kid to understand that what you're doing is giving them attention, then what you're actually doing becomes less important. Of course kids want their needs met, but what is their most basic need? To be tended to.

The Relationship Checkup:
The Importance of Content and Process

Did your own dad ever sit down and ask for your feedback about how things were going between you two or listen to your ideas for how he could improve his fathering? What both Jonah and Hannah learned from the answers, or the content, is important; equally if not more significant, however, is the very action, or process, of doing such an exercise. Jonah said, for example, how afterward both he and Hannah agreed it was good to put words to their actions. Just making the time and doing the Relationship Checkup will speak volumes to your child about how seriously you take your role as a dad and how important she is to you and will make clear that talking to each other is part of what relationships are about.

For any dad — including dads with adult children, as you will see in the excerpt from Bill and Will below — to initiate the Relationship Checkup can be challenging. The kind of resistance that Hannah put up is par for the course for children and teens. I don't know too many young people who get excited by the idea of discussing their relationship with their dad. Yet once Jonah helped push through it — not by fighting but by acknowledging his daughter's disinterest — she agreed and ultimately found it to be a positive experience. Bill and Will's story can be seen as an echo of Jonah's story, a cautionary tale about the consequences of not pushing through and starting this dialogue early; yet, these two stories, as you will see below, are similar in that they show that generational legacies can be stopped, started, and changed at any point in the life of a dad, daughter, or son.

EXERCISE 14. The Modern Dad's Relationship Checkup: Excerpts from Will and Bill

Will's Responses

1. Something I really enjoy doing with you is: *Talking about ideas and philosophies and comedy.*
2. One of the best things you've done for me lately is: *Send me an unsolicited letter laying bare parts of your past and personality I had never known about. Best gift ever.*

3. **A way that I think we're similar is:** *We are both intellectual and creative souls who love to make others laugh.*

4. **A way that I think we're different is:** *You are staunchly conservative and uptight about more things than you would freely admit. I am far more liberal and anti–Catholic Church doctrine than I have ever freely admitted to you.*

5. **A subject I find difficult to talk about with you is:** *Drugs and alcohol. You've become such a puritan and so anxiety ridden about addiction befalling you or one of your kids (an unfounded fear — just look at how well we all turned out!), that we never feel comfortable even talking about, let alone indulging in, our drink or drug of choice in your presence. So we always hid our drinking or drugging from you, which, ironically, is addictive behavior — the very thing you feared.*

6. **A subject I think you find difficult to talk about with me is:** *The truth of who you were and who your family was when you were a kid, an adolescent, a young adult.*

7. **Ways that I sometimes make our relationship difficult are:** *Avoidance. Sometimes I don't want a huge hassle or a long conversation or a deep talk. So I blow you off. Our correspondence often takes on the weight of a John and John Quincy Adams. Historical and brilliant. Everything needs to be eloquently worded for posterity's sake. High-minded, and thought provoking, and soul stirring, and flowery, and effusive — and sometimes it all makes me want to gag. It's so heavy-handed and phony sounding. Even though I know it's really not phony with you, it's still a burden. It's effortful. So I dodge calls. Or delay responding to emails because it'll take so long to respond appropriately.*

8. **Ways that you sometimes make our relationship difficult are:** *Not being real. Keeping our dealings so high-minded that they become very surface level and not real. You don't fully know the real me.*

9. **One way that I can strengthen our relationship is:** *Giving you what I want from you: Honesty. Realness. Sharing.*

10. **One way that you can strengthen our relationship is:** *Honesty. Realness. Sharing. Not judging.*
11. **One of my greatest fears is:** *Failure. Not being the best.*
12. **I think one of your greatest fears is:** *That one of your kids will become a bad drinker.*
13. **Something I need more of from you is:** *Financial guidance.*
14. **In the next six months, I want us to:** *Talk about an R-rated comedy movie I really like and have you not be a negative, stodgy, judgmental puritan about it.*
15. **If today were our last day together, one thing I would want to make sure you know is:** *You are my hero. My idol. You are everything I want to be. I am so lucky to have such a great dad, such a loving mentor, such a centered and decent and spiritual guy. People would kill to have a dad like you. And I squander the resource I have in you far too often. Sometimes I feel unworthy of you — I fear that I am not going to be as great a father as you were, that I will be too caught up in work and trying to succeed in this tough business I chose and that my family life will suffer for it. And I know that in your eyes, that would be the greatest failure of all. To forget my priorities. To let work come before family. And to have unhappy kids or a broken marriage because of it. That's my biggest fear — not living up to the sterling example you provided.*

Bill Sr.'s Responses

1. **Something I really enjoy doing with you is:** *Will, I enjoy just being with you. On a walk, on a golf course, in a car, at a restaurant — just being with you, listening to you, sharing with you, discussing fatherhood, faith, family, friends, books, movies, hopes, dreams, fears — all of it.*
2. **One of the best things you've done for me lately is:** *To connect so intimately and so honestly in writing, on the phone, and in person. Also, opening your heart and your home and sharing*

Anne and Liam and Isla means so much more to me than I could ever say.

3. **A way that I think we're similar is:** *We're very similar in many ways, as your beautiful wife often notes. One way that occurs to me is that we're both driven. We apprehend the good, we set our sights, and we go for it.*

4. **A way that I think we're different is:** *You have displayed a penchant for summoning higher levels of courage and perseverance as evinced by your most impressive pursuit of a much more challenging, much less traditional path.*

5. **A subject I find difficult to talk about with you is:** *I suppose any emotionally charged issue or personal failing is difficult, but I desperately want to override these fears. One memory floats up: when you were thirteen and I, at your mother's insistence, had The Talk with you. You sat in the front seat next to me. As we drove through the streets of New Milford, I told you that it was time to have the talk. You stared straight ahead in obvious discomfort. Of course, I couldn't begin in a serious manner as a normal father would. I said something such as: Will, it's time for me to speak with you about where babies come from, and the truth is that a stork brings them. Your response couldn't have been more vintage: Dad, I'm really glad that we could have this talk. Again, whatever subject I find difficult to speak with you about, I would love to address, conquer what I must.*

6. **A subject I think you find difficult to talk about with me is:** *I don't know that you find too many subjects difficult to talk about. I think it's just difficult for you to find time to talk. You are so incredibly busy. As impressive as your drive is, and as trite as it sounds, I fear that too often you can slip into being a human doing instead of a human being.*

7. **Ways that I sometimes make our relationship difficult are:** *By having been the world's superego. As colleagues have said, I'm not an easy person to share bad news with. For all the negative*

consequences that come from my having erected and maintained this powerful shield, this reverse force field, I am truly sorry.

8. **Ways that you sometimes make our relationship difficult are:** It has been said that when I want to shut someone off, I do so with tremendous force. The door is slammed in the face. I believe that you have learned this behavior well.

9. **One way that I can strengthen our relationship is:** By telling the truth. My expression of open, honest truth will strengthen our relationship, Will.

10. **One way that you can strengthen our relationship is:** Your continued expression of truth will continue to strengthen our relationship.

11. **One of my greatest fears is:** That you won't slow down enough to let your back heal and get healthy and to maintain your health.

12. **I think one of your greatest fears is:** That you won't chase the dream energetically enough to find the level of success you desire.

13. **Something I need more of from you is:** To let me in and to share with me all the ways in which I can help you.

14. **In the next six months, I want us to:** Be fully with each other in any way possible.

15. **If today were our last day together, one thing I would want to make sure you know is:** I love you with all my heart. I could not be more proud of you. For choosing your career, for choosing and loving Anne, for fathering Liam and Isla, for mentoring Dan and Matt and Sam, for being such a great and loving son, for being such a loyal friend to so many, for being such an intellectual Catholic man of faith and honor. I love you for the full beauty and truth of who you are, Will.

Bill Sr.'s Reflections on Doing the Relationship Checkup

BILL: What we most want, we often push away from us. However unwittingly, I have done so in my relationships. Will's responses to the exercise have helped me to see and accept, and to strive to learn from and correct, the truth of my way of being. By having worked so hard at breaking cycles of generations of family dysfunction, at becoming — in an almost Gatsby-like fashion — a new man, a larger-than-life, way too high-minded figure, a truly great "somebody," I have morphed into this difficult-to-approach, impossible-to-emulate fa-cade of a person with whom it is very hard to share openly and hon-estly and intimately. Denying the past doesn't work. Laying bare the truth surely does.

All this is perhaps a bit overstated. Will expressed mostly love and admiration and respect, but he did indeed expose less than sa-vory truths. He admitted that it has been exhausting to live with a tremendously popular public man, and he has helped me under-stand, more intimately, that the same is true for me. It's okay to kick back and relax and let my guard down and stop doing, doing, doing and start just being and knowing — truly knowing and therefore lov-ing my son and myself and every other struggling soul on God's green earth. What a gift!

Will Burke's Reflections
on Doing the Relationship Checkup

WILL: This exercise truly brought us closer together. The most poignant part for me was to realize that my dad is just a person. For the first time in my life, I saw him as a peer — as a sum total of his life experiences and decisions — and it made me so grateful he had made so many good decisions that directly benefited me. In listing my dad's faults, I began to recognize some of the same (and some different) failings in myself. And I am working already on correcting those.

It has been most meaningful to hear about my father's fears for me. This is nothing he has ever or would have ever shared with me. He's afraid I will become the cliché of a human doing rather than a human being. I think about that every day, as I strive to carve out a more relaxed life in which I have a better balance between family time and work time.

Key Lessons from Using the Relationship Checkup

The responses and reflections of Bill and Will, and Jonah and Hannah, illustrate both how this practical tool can be used and the powerful impact it can have on all dad-child relationships, no matter how old the dad or the child is. Below are key lessons to take away from the above reflections, and more universally about the experiences of the many dads, sons, and daughters who have used the Relationship Checkup (on their own, in one of my workshops or retreats, or in another setting). Using the Relationship Checkup will help:

- *Teach your children to have high standards for relationships.* How we treat our children from an early age becomes a standard for how they expect to be treated in all their relationships, from friendships to dating to marriage. By encouraging your daughter to address problems directly with you — despite her fear — you teach her not to silence herself in any relationship. By listening to your son's feelings, you teach him to expect others to be present for him as well. By respecting their individuality and point of view, you teach your children to insist on being treated well by others.
- *Build trust by staying accountable for the job you do as a dad.* We don't often think of adults needing to be accountable to children. But if we want our children to trust and respect us, staying accountable — taking responsibility for the effect of our words and actions — is essential. A dad who rages at his children can stay accountable by getting help. A dad who rarely sees his children (because of work,

a separation, etc.) can stay accountable by letting his children know that he understands their pain or anger. The tricky thing about staying accountable to a child is that we don't always know how our behavior affects them; they won't necessarily say, "Your anger really frightens me." In fact, they're more likely to remain silent and take it out on themselves or others. The Relationship Checkup provides a structured way for children to tell us how well we're handling our job as dads.

It is a father's responsibility to ensure that a child feels safe to speak up in the father-child relationship. If the child does not feel safe, either out of a fear of retribution for speaking his or her truth or fear that the father won't be able to tolerate what she or he has to say, then trust will be very difficult, if not impossible, to build. Listening to our children's experience of us as fathers does not mean we abdicate our responsibility to set firm, consistent limits. Setting limits is how *we* keep our children accountable to *us*.

Being accountable to a child should not be confused with parents giving up their authority. Just because a child says that she thinks you don't give her enough freedom and independence doesn't mean you remove her curfew. To the contrary, this kind of request from a child can become a point of curiosity for further discussion: "What do you mean by freedom? How much freedom do you think you can handle? How will we know?" Dialogue builds trust; unquestionable authority foments rebellion.

Similarly, the Relationship Checkup is *not* about becoming friends with our children. The key difference is that we don't place our needs on a child as we would on a friend or partner. There is nothing burdening about letting a child know that you intend to get your anger under control or that you are concerned about how much time you spend at work. By the same token, there is nothing burdening about letting a child know how much joy and meaning he or she brings to your life.

Accountability ultimately breeds intimacy and connection. By bringing our children's voice and experience into our relationship, we teach them that speaking up for what they want and need in a relationship is vital, that they are valuable and worthy of listening to, and that we are fallible. Then they do not grow up thinking of their father, and by extension men in general, as unreachable, unknowable, or unaccountable.

- *Teach children the foundations of relationship literacy.* When you were young, how did you learn about relationships? Maybe you watched the adults in your home or friends' homes, learned from TV, movies, and health class, or took in some teachings through your religion. Chances are you didn't receive much formal instruction. Today most children are not taught relationship skills in any comprehensive way. The Relationship Checkup emphasizes the foundations of emotional literacy: self-reflection, giving and receiving feedback, getting your needs met, and listening, to name just a few.

- *Model the disappearing art of reflection.* In this age of email, IM, Twitter, and Facebook, it's easy for children to react without thinking, to reveal too much about themselves too quickly, and to develop a false sense of connection with someone they may not know very well. The Relationship Checkup teaches them to slow down and reflect on themselves and their relationships.

How to Get Started

Now that you've seen how the Relationship Checkup works, it is important to think through how to apply this to *your* relationship. Carefully read through the versions of the Relationship Checkup and determine which would work best for you and your child (given age, maturity, current state of your relationship, etc.). In some cases, especially with younger children or a child for whom attention is an issue, sitting with them as you go through the questions may be necessary. If writing is a problem, you can still have a child quietly reflect, even doodle or draw. The key is taking time and giving thought to the questions.

Getting more specific, it is very important to think through when and where you will do the Relationship Checkup and how you can make it special. The Relationship Checkup should be done outside the home. Consider taking a drive or a walk, sitting in a park, or having a meal at a quiet restaurant. Make sure there is enough privacy for your child to feel comfortable talking: a baseball game, a crowded café, or a mall would be too distracting and would most likely defeat the purpose. However, to make this a special event, you could go to a movie, a game, or the mall after taking the Checkup.

Finally, when you introduce the idea to your child, you should expect resistance. Think about Jonah's story, how he didn't fight Hannah's initial complaints, kept going, and clearly acknowledged it was something he was asking of her (as if asking a favor of her). Describe the Relationship Checkup and your ideas for making it a special event. Ask for his ideas. You may be met with some resistance, especially from a teenager. Explain that it's very easy to do, that it would mean a lot to you, and that he'll have a good time. When younger children resist, emphasize the fun part; with older children, emphasize how important they are to you, how time

flies, and how you want to make the most of it. If necessary, use a
food/fun bribe. As a last resort, make it mandatory, just as you
would any other family obligation. If you are met with a great deal
of resistance or think it would be better to ease into doing the
Checkup, you can select just a portion of the questions. I recommend selecting some questions from each section. Also, I encourage you to eventually do the entire Checkup in one sitting.

Finally, remember that ultimately this is about building, strength-
ening, your emotional connection with your child. If you feel it's
already strong, the exercise will serve as an affirmation. Stepping
into any discomfort you may have initiating this kind of dialogue
is, as you saw in both stories above, an essential form of courage
that is necessary to realizing your vision of a close, connected, and
healthy relationship with your children. Being a dad is not just
something you are; it's also something you do.

The Relationship Checkup Four Years Later

As a way to illustrate how the Relationship Checkup is intended to be
used over time, as well as how certain themes remain constant and
others change in any father-child relationship, below I have provided
an excerpt of Jonah's and Hannah's recent responses to the Relationship Checkup. Remember, in the excerpt above she was nine, and here
she is thirteen. Most significantly, you will see how again Hannah re-
sists initially doing the Relationship Checkup — as does Jonah find
more challenge in initiating it — but also admits how meaningful this
dialogue with her dad truly is; her response to the last question is

15. In the next six months, I want us to:
     *Be at a complete understanding of where the other is at
     in life: what their worries are, their fears, their hopes, their
     achievements.*

EXERCISE 14. **The Modern Dad's Relationship Checkup Four Years Later: Excerpts from Jonah and Hannah (age thirteen)**

Jonah's Responses

1. The positive qualities that I bring to our relationship are:
   I am firm but loving.
   I am clear with boundaries and the reasons for them.
   I am open to questions and answering them honestly.
   I am open to criticism and taking it in a healthy way.
   I am honest about admitting when I'm wrong.
   I am fun and playful.
   I am doing activities like this one that encourage communication.

2. The positive qualities that you bring to the relationship are:
   You are thoughtful.
   You are articulate.
   You are hard-working.
   You are honest.
   You are don't stay mad at me too long.
   You are open to questions and criticisms.

3. Ways that I sometimes make our relationship difficult are:
   I am disorganized.
   I am grumpy.
   I get stressed easily when I don't need to.
   I travel too much.
   I try to help too much, not giving you your space to learn on your own.
   I am condescending, treating you like you're younger than you are.

4. Ways that you sometimes make our relationship difficult are:
   You get frustrated with me when I'm trying to help.
   You take my time and energy for granted.

You are not ready when you say you will be.
You forget things.
You don't take care of your stuff.
You shut down/withhold affection when you don't get what
    you want.

5. One way I can strengthen our relationship is:
   By being better about being helpful in general (waiting to be asked, not just doing it for you, etc.).

6. One way that you can strengthen our relationship is:
   By being more realistic about time, especially when it involves me driving or something.

7. A subject I find difficult to talk about with you is:
   Boys, kissing, sex, etc.

8. A subject I think you find difficult to talk about with me is:
   Boys, kissing, sex, etc.

9. One of my greatest fears is:
   That you won't tell me if you get in a dangerous/unhealthy situation because you're scared I'll be mad or judge you.

10. I think one of your greatest fears is:
    That I'll be lonely or sad if I don't marry someone again.

11. I think one of the best things you've done for me is:
    Shown me the value of commitment.

12. I think one of the best things I have done for you is:
    Been myself, followed my dreams, and worked hard for them while still being a good father, balancing things I love.

13. A way that I think we're similar is:
    We love playing and running around.

14. A way that I think we're different is:
    I like talking about stuff (emotions, etc.) more.

15. In the next six months, I want us to:
    Go running together, take a nice trip somewhere, play some sports together, stay in touch about how you're feeling growing up and how I'm feeling watching you (and growing up myself).

Hannah's Responses

1. Positive qualities that I bring to our relationship are:
   Joyfulness (most of the time), responsibility, and awareness.
2. Positive qualities that you bring to the relationship are:
   Honesty, respect for my privacy, tolerance and patience for when I mess up or make mistakes, tolerance and patience for driving me all around the city, always offering (if not too much) to help with anything I need or ask for, just being there to talk, letting me know of the real reality of certain situations, sincerity, understanding, and relatability.
3. Ways that I sometimes make our relationship difficult are:
   Not wanting to talk or open up about things, my lack of time-understanding, the grudges I try to hold, my unloving attitude when I'm mad or upset, when I act selfish and don't think about the people around me, my self-consciousness of not impressing you or mom, not wanting to spend as much time with you as I should.
4. Ways that you sometimes make our relationship difficult are:
   High expectations, giving me help when I didn't ask for it or don't need it, little mood swings (only sometimes, and I have them too), your sensitivity and stubbornness.
5. One way I can strengthen our relationship is:
   Talking to you about things that are bothering me or that are just on my mind.
6. One way that you can strengthen our relationship is:
   Remembering that even though I act embarrassed of you sometimes, or ask to spend time with my friends during "our" weekends, I still love you.
7. A subject I find difficult to talk about with you is:
   Boys.
8. A subject I think you find difficult to talk about with me is:
   Absolutely nothing!
9. One of my greatest fears is:

My parents dying or me not being accepted by those I love and care about.

10. **I think one of your greatest fears is:**
    Messing up.

11. **I think one of the best things you've done for me is:**
    Let me appreciate the little things in life, like our drives by the ocean or our times playing Wii and watching The Office together.

12. **I think one of the best things I have done for you is:**
    Helped you to be more responsible and think about the consequences of your actions.

13. **A way that I think we're similar is:**
    Our looks (ha-ha) and our sense of humor.

14. **A way that I think we're different is:**
    You can be more sentimental than me.

15. **In the next six months, I want us to:**
    Be at a complete understanding of where the other is at in life: what their worries are, their fears, their hopes, their achievements.

Conclusion

In my early twenties I was confused about which career path to follow. I recall feeling very envious of my best friend, Jonah, who had known since a young age that he wanted to be a musician. I told him how lucky he was to have such clarity about his future. His response has always stuck with me: "The difficult part about knowing what I want is that I'm painfully aware of when I'm not going after it. I feel a sense of responsibility to make my dreams a reality."

My hope is that as you finish this book you will feel that same sense of responsibility toward realizing a new vision of fatherhood. As modern dads we have a gift that most of our fathers did not: that of knowing what a tremendous difference we can make in our children's lives. We see it in the research, we hear about it from the women in our lives, and we feel it in our hearts: children need to feel close and connected, to feel "at home" in their relationship with their fathers. They need a new kind of provider, a dad who supports them not only materially but also emotionally, physically, and spiritually. This is a tall order indeed.

Realizing this vision and delivering for our children, our families, and the next generation of dads require stepping out of our fathers' footsteps and onto a new road, the road connecting our work life to our family life, our head to our heart, our desire to achieve with our need to just be. In short, it's the road that leads back home.

My own father was not expected to walk this road. Home, literally and figuratively, was a woman's domain. The so-called feminine qualities, such as caretaking, emotionality, and empathy, held little value in his world. We now know that these human qualities not only enrich our family's lives but also help us live longer. According to Dr. Eli Newberger, the messages boys and men get to go it alone or not ask for help are major contributing factors in why men die on average five years earlier than women.[1] In contrast, men who experience intimacy and connection in their lives are healthier than men who do not.

Modern fatherhood is about filling your life with healthy practices: showing up for your children and partner, learning new skills, building support networks, and measuring success by the quality and health of your relationships. The vision is clear, and the road is before us. Now we must each bear responsibility for becoming the modern dad our children and families need us to be.

I hope that you continue to use this book as a reference. But whether or not you do, it's critical that you develop some form of ongoing support. Choose one or more of the suggestions, and set a realistic goal for getting the kind of support that will work best for you.

1. *Develop male friendships.* Periodically get together with one of your male friends to check in about fatherhood, relationships, your work life, and so on. This may require you to initiate discussions and to put your own issues right on

the table, but it will also take your friendships to a deeper level. Remember, it's good for our children when we model healthy male friendships. It can also lighten the emotional load many of us place on the women in our lives.

2. *Attend a dads' group or men's group.* Look for a supportive, activity-based, skills-oriented, or discussion-based group. Some groups are more formal, such as those done in therapeutic settings or through your religious affiliation. Others are more casual, such as a group of dads who work (or play sports) together and have dinner every few weeks to talk about fatherhood and family life. Schools are a great resource for parenting. These days many more schools have fathers' groups. If the school does not have anything for dads, start a modern dads' group yourself (email john@john badalament.com for tips on starting one).

3. *Talk with your partner or with a like-minded couple.* Commit to regular discussions with your partner or with another like-minded couple about parenting, relationship issues, and so on.

4. *Find a good therapist or other community resource.* Depending on where you live, a professional therapist is a good option for exploring fatherhood and relationship issues. Community resources may include religious organizations, local health centers, Boys and Girls Clubs, YMCA organizations, and so forth.

The practice of fathering is like staying physically fit; it takes consistent knowledge, awareness, and action.

I think one of the best ways for modern dads to learn about fathering is by getting together with other dads. I'm not talking about joining a men's support group. I mean finding two or three other dads (friends, co-workers, etc.) and making time to get together informally and talk about being a dad. The simplest model is for each guy to take about ten or fifteen minutes to talk about something that went well for him as a dad (and as a husband or partner) recently and a moment he wishes he could do over.

Amazingly enough, in contemporary American society for a group of men to sit together and simply speak the truth — about ourselves and our relationships — is a revolutionary act. This is especially true when we get together across lines of race, ethnicity, culture, and class. I believe dads are hungry for such forums.

Men's organizations, religious communities, therapeutic settings, recovery programs, human service agencies, some school communities, and the occasional progressive community of parents often provide these forums. But by and large, for most modern dads there is likely very little space in their social lives to talk with other dads about their day-to-day experiences of fatherhood, let alone the deeper emotional, spiritual, and relationship issues. So many dads remain unnecessarily cut off from one of the richest, most influential, and most powerful shapers of our experience of fatherhood.

This book is meant to provide a kind of forum. I hope that it will inspire you to get together with other dads — and with moms too. In no way do I intend to encourage modern dads to claim parenthood as their own territory and to shut women out; on the contrary, this book is about men speaking with one another and with women about their fears, joys, stories, and truths. It is about men bringing their experience of modern fatherhood — in all its complexity — to the forefront of their relationships.

Exercises

This appendix consists of practical skill-building exercises to do by yourself, with your children, and, in some cases, with your partner or close friend. These are the same exercises — in their full form — that I gave to the dads featured in this book to complete. These exercises are sequenced to build on one another. Viewed as a whole, they present a complete and clear vision for modern fatherhood.

EXERCISE 1 • CHAPTER ONE • PAGE 21

Dad's Vision Statement
Prepare to Write Your Dad's Vision Statement

Imagine twenty years from now your child is approached to be in a documentary film about fathers. Now imagine the filmmaker asks your child to describe his/her relationship with you. With this in mind, respond to the questions below:

1. **Describe three things you hope your child would say to the film-maker about his/her relationship with you.**
    Examples may include: "I hope my child would say she felt that I really valued her opinion even if I didn't agree with it," or "I hope my child would say that he learned respect for women by watching me."

    1. _____
    _____
    2. _____
    _____
    3. _____
    _____

2. **Describe three things you hope your child would not say about his/her relationship with you.**
    Examples may include, "I hope my child would not say that our relationship was one of image and not substance. My dad did all the right things but I never felt connected with him," or "I hope my child would not say that I was a terrible listener."

    1. _____
    _____
    2. _____
    _____
    3. _____
    _____

Write Your Dad's Vision Statement

Your Dad's Vision Statement will guide you in developing the kind of relationship you want with your child. It will help you make important choices and set forth your priorities in your relationship. Please do the following:

Reflect on your responses to Exercise 1. Then choose two from each list (what you hope they say and don't say) that are the most important/challenging for you and fill in below.

Twenty years from now, I hope my child says . . .

Twenty years from now, I hope my child does not say . . .

Today my priorities are . . .

What I need to change . . .

Fulfill Your Dad's Vision Statement

What skills, knowledge, and support do you need to be the father that you want to be for your family? If you have trouble, ask your partner or someone you trust what he or she thinks.

SKILLS

_____

_____

_____

KNOWLEDGE

_____

_____

_____

SUPPORT

_____

_____

_____

Find a Witness

In order to have some accountability and support in realizing your Dad's Vision Statement, it's important to have a witness. Find someone close to you (another dad, a friend, your partner, etc.) with whom you would feel comfortable discussing your Dad's Vision Statement.

WHOM I PLAN TO TALK TO: _____

WHEN I WILL TALK TO THEM: _____

EXERCISE 2 • CHAPTER TWO • PAGE 42

Identify the Gifts and Liabilities from Your Father

Below is a list of gifts your father may have given you and liabilities he may have left you with. (Circle) as many as apply to your relationship with your father. Feel free to add any gifts or liabilities that are not on the list but apply to you.

GIFTS	LIABILITIES
A good work ethic	Often or completely absent
Instilled sense of security/family	Didn't control anger
Faced down adversity	Deceptive
Warm, caring, loving	Overly critical
Kept in touch consistently	Couldn't tolerate vulnerability
Showed humility	Avoided conflict
Assertiveness	Wouldn't talk about feelings
Showed up to events	Workaholic
Shared family stories	Addiction to alcohol/drugs
Empathy	Unwilling to ask for help
Handled conflict responsibly	Uninvolved in daily parenting
An active and involved parent	Kept up appearances
Respected women as equals	Rarely showed up at events
A good listener	Sexist attitudes toward women
Expressed individuality and passion	Blamed others for his problems
Self-assured and confident	Lacked self-confidence
Valued diversity	Cast a big shadow
Treated others kindly	Disrespectful to others
Spirituality	Didn't stand up for himself
Involved in community life	No consequences for his actions

EXERCISE 3 • CHAPTER TWO • PAGE 44

Bridge the Past and Future

Choose three gifts from the list in Exercise 2 that you want to pass on to your children and fill in the chart below. For example, if your father's gift was that he showed up at all of your games/events, you may be trying to pass this on by rearranging your schedule at work. You will know you're successful by asking your child if they think you show up enough.

GIFTS

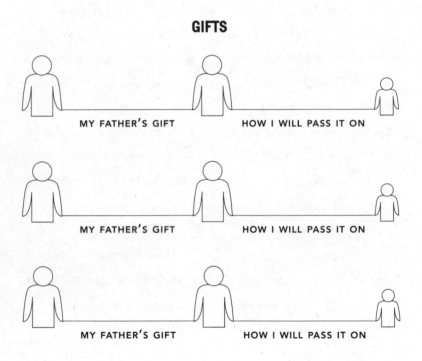

MY FATHER'S GIFT   HOW I WILL PASS IT ON

MY FATHER'S GIFT   HOW I WILL PASS IT ON

MY FATHER'S GIFT   HOW I WILL PASS IT ON

Now choose three liabilities from the list that you're determined not to repeat and fill in the chart below. For example, your father's emotional absence or lack of warmth left you feeling distant as a boy. Today, you may struggle to connect emotionally with your children. You could do differently than your father by reading *Emotional Intelligence* by Daniel Goleman and talking with other dads about how they connect with their children.

LIABILITIES

MY FATHER'S LIABILITY   WHAT I WILL DO DIFFERENTLY

MY FATHER'S LIABILITY   WHAT I WILL DO DIFFERENTLY

MY FATHER'S LIABILITY   WHAT I WILL DO DIFFERENTLY

EXERCISE 4 • CHAPTER TWO • PAGE 52

Explore Your Mother's Legacy

A man's relationship with his mother affects how he will parent his own children. Answer the following questions.

1. What gifts did your mother give you that you intend to pass on to your children?

    _____

    _____

2. What liabilities has she left you that you don't want to give to your children?

    _____

    _____

3. Were there ways she interacted with your father that were healthy and positive?

    _____

    _____

4. Were there ways she interacted with your father that were unhealthy or upsetting to you?

    _____

    _____

5. What messages did she give you about men in general?

    _____

    _____

6. What were the ways she treated you that made you feel good?

    _____

    _____

7. What were the ways she treated you that made you feel bad or uncomfortable?

    _____

    _____

8. How have the women in your life been similar to and/or different from your mother?

    _____

    _____

EXERCISE 5 • CHAPTER TWO • PAGES 59 & 60

Write Three Letters to Your Father

Write the following three letters in order. The exercise is a way to have "the talk" with your father between your own two ears. You may decide to send or read these letters to your father; you may not. You may instead decide to read them to a friend or partner. This activity is more about the *process* of writing the letters. What you do with them is up to you.

 1. Write to your father about what it was like for you growing up with (or without) him. Describe what was positive, as well as what was difficult or negative. Think about the things you've wanted to say to him but never have. You may cover your entire childhood or choose to focus on a particular time period or even a specific incident.

 2. Write *from your father's perspective* (the letter should start with "Dear Son,"). This letter should capture what you imagine your father would say to you in response to letter #1. How would your father react to that letter? Would he accept your point of view? Would he argue certain things? Would he be loving, hurt, or angry? Imagine, as best you can, his response.

 3. Write again *from your father's perspective*. This letter should capture what you hope or wish your father's response would be. In other words, if he were to respond in the best possible way to reading letter #1, what would he say? This letter is a way for you to imagine your father giving you everything you wished he would have given you.

Find a Witness

Understanding the many different ways our parents' legacies affect us is not always easy. Sometimes those connections are clear, for example, when we catch ourselves saying something exactly like our father did; other times we may be blinded to how our father's legacy affects us today. In order to gain more insight about these connections, as well as communicate your intentions to repeat/do differently than your parents, please do the following:

Find someone close to you (another dad, a friend, your partner, etc.) and discuss your responses to the Gifts/Liabilities, Bridging Past/Present and Letters exercises.

Assess Your Level of Involvement in Your Child's School

The following table will help you look specifically at your current level of school involvement. Comparing your involvement in your child's school vs. your father's involvement in your school will quickly highlight the similarities and differences. Simply write in the appropriate number in each of the boxes. When finished, compare the results and decide if you should change your level of participation.

1 = RARELY   2 = SOMETIMES   3 = FREQUENTLY

	YOUR DAD	YOU
Drop off/pick up child		
Parent-teacher conferences		
Volunteer at school		
Parent association meetings		
Parent education events (i.e., speakers)		
Class-level events (i.e., science night)		
Whole-school events (sports, drama, clubs)		
TOTAL		

7 to 11 — You need to do more, get going.

12 to 17 — You're on the right track, keep going.

18 to 21 — You're actively involved, good going.

EXERCISE 7 • CHAPTER THREE • PAGE 78

Take a Snapshot of Housework and Childcare Responsibilities in Your Family

The following exercise is intended to raise your awareness about the division of labor in your family. If you are in a two-parent family, pay attention to the balance of responsibilities between you and your partner. Even if your partner stays at home, it is important to model some degree of equality. Children need to learn that men's work at home is not limited to stereotypical tasks such as taking out the garbage and paying the bills. If you are a single dad who does everything on these lists, take a moment to think about where you may find more support.

Take an inventory of child- and home-related tasks by circling a dot on the scale.

CHILD-RELATED TASKS	MOSTLY DAD	ABOUT EVEN	MOSTLY MOM
Purchases your children's clothes?	• • • • •		
Schedules doctor's appointments?	• • • • •		
Makes childcare arrangements?	• • • • •		
Bathes and gets younger kids ready for bed?	• • • • •		
Arranges social plans such as play dates?	• • • • •		
Monitors curfews of older children?	• • • • •		
Checks in with your older children?	• • • • •		
Sets limits with the children?	• • • • •		
Maintains contact with your child's school?	• • • • •		

HOUSE-RELATED TASKS	MOSTLY DAD		ABOUT EVEN		MOSTLY MOM
Does the laundry and cleans house?	●	●	●	●	●
Takes out the garbage?	●	●	●	●	●
Cleans the bathrooms?	●	●	●	●	●
Makes lunches?	●	●	●	●	●
Makes the beds?	●	●	●	●	●
Vacuums and dusts?	●	●	●	●	●
Does outside maintenance?	●	●	●	●	●
Makes sure the children do their chores?	●	●	●	●	●
Does the food shopping?	●	●	●	●	●
Cooks family meals?	●	●	●	●	●
Cleans up after family meals?	●	●	●	●	●
Does the finances?	●	●	●	●	●
Buys gifts and writes thank-you notes?	●	●	●	●	●

EXERCISE 8 • CHAPTER FOUR • PAGE 112

Create Ritual Dad Time

Guidelines

1. **Get together as father/child at least once a month.** Minimally for at least one to two hours and with only one child at a time (this may be difficult for larger families, but it is essential for building a one-on-one relationship).
2. **Choose an activity you both agree on.** You may allow your child to choose or alternate who decides. I don't recommend executive decisions, except in cases of extreme resistance (more on that below).
3. **Make sure you talk during your time together.** Going to a movie or a game is fine. Using what William Pollack (author of *Real Boys*) calls "action talk" (i.e., shooting baskets or playing video games while talking) is great, but as men we also need to model face-to-face dialogue for children of all ages. We don't always need a distraction! Every three to four months, use your Ritual Dad Time to do the Relationship Checkup.
4. **Be consistent.** The ritual does not have to be on the same day each month, but make sure it happens so your child can count on it. I suggest scheduling your next ritual time at the end of each time together.

Examples include: Going for a meal, taking a walk, visiting another town, going for a bike ride, cooking a meal from a foreign country, working on a building/fix-it project, taking a drive, going to a sporting event, playing a game, doing an art project, etc.

For live-away dads: Depending on how often you see your child, either your ritual may be done less frequently (every three, six, or twelve months) or you could do a long-distance ritual, such as a monthly letter or ongoing project.

For dads with infants or newborns: Think about visiting different environments that may stimulate your child's different senses, such as a park with a lot of birds, the beach, a crowded playground, a quiet forest, live or recorded music, etc.

Make the Pitch to Your Child

Make the pitch to your child and expect some resistance. Express that you would like to try this once a month for six months. I suggest that you make this a request on your part, something *you* are asking of *your child*. For example, a father I know told his eleventh-grade daughter that he wanted to have time with her before she went to college; on the face of it, she would be doing this for him. Also, make it clear that you have no other agenda than to have fun and spend time doing things they want to do on a regular basis: call it a bribe or just a nice offer.

If met with total resistance, I advocate making it mandatory. That's right, mandatory. The resentment and resistance will almost certainly fade. I once prescribed this ritual time for a father and teenage son who were constantly in conflict with each other. Part of their problem was that they had too few positive experiences together. Younger kids will be far less likely to resist.

Finally, it's important to let your child's mother know what you're doing up front. This will reduce the likelihood of her having any resistance. Explain what you're doing and why this ritual time is so important. Also, listen to and take her concerns seriously. On the positive side, she may offer some good suggestions or tips as well. Keep your child's mother in the loop.

Brainstorm some possible rituals:

_____

_____

_____

_____

_____

_____

_____

_____

_____

_____

_____

_____

Keep a Log of Your Ritual Dad Time

You can use the space provided in the Handbook or use your own journal. The idea is to reflect on the experience each time, if only briefly. Think about what went well, things you discussed, what didn't go well, etc. Plan on doing your ritual for at least six consecutive months. If after the first or second month your ritual time is not going well, consider the following:

- Are you giving your child a choice about how the time is spent?
- Are you totally present during your time together (not talking on the cell phone, not stopping to run errands, not having the TV on)?
- Talk with your child's mother or a friend about what is happening and ask for their suggestions.
- Talk with your child about ideas for what you could do to improve your time together.

Since you are initiating the ritual it's important to first look at your own behavior and see what you could change.

DESCRIBE YOUR RITUAL:

DATE:

WHAT WE DID:

MY REFLECTIONS:

NEXT RITUAL TIME (WHAT/WHEN):

EXERCISE 9 • CHAPTER FIVE • PAGE 116

Take the Modern Dad's Quiz:
How Well Do You Know Your Children?

Most of us think we know our kids pretty well, sometimes even better than they know themselves, right? Well, in order to test our knowledge, I have developed a short quiz for dads to take. For some, this will be simple; if so, consider it an affirmation of what a great parent you are. For others, especially dads with limited contact with their children, this will be a more difficult exercise; use the quiz as a reminder, motivator, or wake-up call.

Take the following quiz alone. Answer all the questions you can for each of your children. When you finish, check your answers by talking directly with your child, your child's mother, or your partner. Make sure you fill in any questions you got wrong or left blank.

1. What recent accomplishment is your child most proud of?

2. Name one of your child's big disappointments this year.

3. What are your child's current prized possessions?

4. What is your child's favorite food?

5. Can you name your child's teachers?

6. Name two things your child did at school in the past two weeks.

7. What is most challenging about school for your child?

8. What does your child like about school?

9. What does your child like to do in his/her spare time?

10. What types of music does your child listen to?

11. Which TV shows, movies, actors/characters, and athletes are popular with your child and his/her friends?

12. What are his/her three favorite websites?

13. Does your child belong to any social networking websites (MySpace, Facebook, Club Penguin, etc.)?

14. What causes your child the greatest stress?

15. Who are your child's close friends, and why does he/she like them?

16. Who are your child's heroes and role models?

17. What would your child like to be when he/she grows up?

18. What is something that really upsets your child?

19. What does your child like to do with you?

20. What does your child love about you?

EXERCISE 10 • CHAPTER FIVE • PAGE 130

Explore Different Ways to Get Involved at School

This action will help you discover the range of ways you could be involved and, more importantly, what your child's school needs from you and other dads. Chances are you could be more involved in your child's school experience. Or maybe it's how you're involved that needs to change. Instead of attending conferences and sporting events, maybe you want to attend a parent night or volunteer your skills. If you are absolutely doing a great job already, this action will serve to increase your knowledge about your child's school.

Now it's time to go on a fact-finding mission. In order to learn about the many ways dads can get involved at school, do all four of the actions in the chart below.

Talk with at least 3 other dads about what they do (or know about). These might be dads you already know or you may step out and meet some new ones.

TEACHERS

Meet or talk with your child's teacher or a school administrator about ways they've seen dads get more involved and what needs they have.

OTHER DADS **PTA MEETINGS**

Talk with your child's mother (if not possible, a mother you know) about dad involvement from the mom's perspective. Is it important? Would it be welcomed?

MOTHER

Attend a PTO/PA meeting at least once. Find out about activities and events in which you could participate. Pay attention to the number of dads present.

IDEAS:

_____
_____
_____
_____
_____
_____
_____
_____
_____
_____
_____
_____
_____
_____
_____
_____
_____
_____
_____
_____
_____
_____
_____

EXERCISE 11 • CHAPTER FIVE • PAGE 140

Identify Your Listening Style:
The Four Kinds of Listeners

Along with your child, review the following descriptions of the four kinds of listeners and discuss which one(s) you most relate to. Then ask your child to assign a percentage indicating how often you become that type of listener with him or her; at the same time rate yourself. Finally, compare your responses together. Optional: Do the same exercise with your wife/partner or friend.

The Journalist

If there is one kind of listener who would be a good default, it's the Journalist. The Journalist asks good questions, some open-ended ("How are things with your friends?"), others closed ("Did you have a good time?"). Her body language lets the speaker know she is tuned in. She makes eye contact and nods, and her facial expressions reflect the speaker's words. She clarifies what the speaker says with an occasional "Is that right?" She also listens for what's not being said. The result is that the speaker feels very attended to, taken care of, and focused on. Young children, especially, need you to be the Journalist.

I am this type of listener ___ percent of the time.

The Storyteller

The Storyteller relates to what the other person is saying by sharing similar stories. Sharing experiences can be a great way to show empathy, that you really "get it." However, if you start telling stories as the listener, it's easy for the speaker to feel that you're more interested in yourself than you are in him.

I am this type of listener ____ percent of the time.

The Vacationer

The Vacationer is not really present for the speaker. Though he may appear to be listening, he is actually vacationing in his mind — thinking about work, somewhere he'd rather be, or the score of the ball game. This kind of listening can be great if the speaker simply wants to spew words or just talk at someone (who could be anyone). However, most people don't like talking to someone who is not really there. Usually, a speaker can tell when she is talking to a Vacationer.

I am this type of listener ____ percent of the time.

The Handyman

This is the kind of listener, stereotypically speaking, that guys tend to like. The Handyman is useful. He's ready to fix any problem. He nods and listens intently, mainly with an ear toward what he can offer. The advantage of the Handyman is that sometimes people want to hear solutions. On the downside, sometimes people just want to be heard, not fixed.

I am this type of listener ____ percent of the time.

EXERCISE 12 • CHAPTER SIX • PAGE 155

Find the Right Stories

Each story topic (left column) has a writing prompt next to it. You may choose to write down some of your stories and keep them as a journal for your children. You could also write these stories as letters to your children to help them learn more about you. This is an especially good idea for those with young children. Finally, share at least one story about yourself when you were your child's current age each week until you've completed the list below. If doing this face-to-face is not possible, you may use phone, letters (handwritten or emailed), video (live or recorded), or other creative ways. Consider also using ritual time (see chapter 4) as a venue to share your stories.

STORY TOPIC	WRITING PROMPT
Family relationships	Dinner at my home growing up…
Friendships	When I was young, my friends…
Getting in trouble	I got in trouble for…
School	I was the kind of student who…
Work	The best/worst job I ever had…
Self-esteem	I felt good/bad about myself…

Body image/Puberty	When I looked in the mirror…
Making decisions	I knew it had to be done, but…
Peer pressure/Fitting in	I knew if I didn't…
Competition	My thrill of victory/agony of defeat…
Interests	Nothing excited me more than…
Attraction/Dating	My first crush…
Sex	Something I wish I knew then…
Spirituality	I believe…
Being irresponsible	I can't believe I…
Money	I've learned that money…
Popular culture	I would do anything to listen/see…

EXERCISE 13 • CHAPTER SIX • PAGES 164, 168 & 179

The Modern Dad's Relationship Checkup

The Modern Dad's Relationship Checkup is a series of questions designed to initiate and encourage ongoing dialogue between dads and children. It's a structured way to have a heart-to-heart talk about your lives and your relationship with each other.

Determine which version of the Relationship Checkup you will be using and carefully read through it.

- The Relationship Checkup for Children   Ages 5–10
- The Relationship Checkup for Teens   Ages 11 and up

Each version has its own step-by-step instructions. Follow them closely so each of you gets enough time to speak.

To effectively introduce this activity to your child and make the most of the experience, you'll need a bit of preparation.

1. Think about when and where you will do the Relationship Checkup and how you can make it special.

    The Relationship Checkup should be done outside of the home. Consider taking a drive or a walk, sitting in a park, having a meal at a quiet restaurant, etc. Make sure there is enough privacy so your child will feel comfortable talking: a baseball game, crowded café, or mall will likely be distracting and defeat the purpose. However, to make this a special event, you could go to a movie, a game, or the mall after doing the Relationship Checkup.

2. Introduce the idea to your child and expect resistance.

    Describe the Relationship Checkup and your ideas for making it a special event; ask for his or her ideas. You may get some resistance, especially from a teenager. Explain that it's very easy, it would mean a lot to you, and the child will have a good time. When younger children resist, emphasize the fun part; with older children, emphasize how important they are to you, how time flies, and that you want to make the most of it. If necessary, use a food/fun bribe. As a last resort, require it, just as you would any other family obligation.

Note: If you get a great deal of resistance or think it would be better to ease into it, you can select a portion of the questions and shorten the activity. I recommend selecting some questions from each section. Also, I encourage you to eventually do the entire Relationship Checkup in one sitting.

The Relationship Checkup for Children (Ages 5–10)

Instructions

STEP 1   Together, read aloud all nineteen questions to make sure you both understand what's being asked. Dad must assure his child that it's safe to be honest. Dad must say: "I want you to answer honestly. I promise to listen without getting upset. What you think is important to me."

STEP 2   Split up and write your answers to every question alone. Agree to return in twenty minutes. If writing is problematic or your child needs help, simply talk through your responses.

STEP 3   When done, come back together. Agree on how much time you'll take to share your answers. I suggest at least twenty minutes. If possible, leave it open-ended.

STEP 4   Dad shares his answer to Question #1. Child shares his or her answer to Question #1. Continue alternating responses to each question, in order, until finished. When listening, focus on what's being said, not what you want to say. Use good body language. Don't interrupt or ask too many questions.

Questions

ABOUT OUR LIVES...

1. A really important friend to me is _____ because...

2. I think my friends like me because...

3. Recently, my friends have been talking a lot about...

4. Something that my peers from school (for child) or work (for dad) do that I don't like or don't understand is...

5. Two things I like about school/work are...

6. If I could change one thing at school/work it would be...

7. FOR CHILD: A current event happening in the world today that I am concerned or confused about is...

   FOR DAD: A current event I've been wondering if you've been affected by is...

ABOUT OUR RELATIONSHIP...

8. Two qualities I like about myself are...

9. Two qualities I like about you are...

10. If I could change any two things about myself (attitude, appearance, behavior), I would change...

11. Something I'm very good at is...

12. Something I wish I was better at is...

13. Something I think you're very good at is...

14. FOR CHILD: Dad, when you were my age, were you...

    FOR DAD: When I was your age, I...

15. FOR CHILD: Something I've always wanted to know about our family (today or in the past) is...

    FOR DAD: Something I liked about my family life growing up and something that was challenging...

16. One of the nicest things you've done for me recently is...

17. One thing I could do to be a better child/dad is...

18. One thing you could do to be a better dad/child is...

19. I hope that we always...

The Relationship Checkup for Teens

Instructions

STEP 1   Together, read aloud all thirty-three questions to make sure you both understand what's being asked. Dad must assure his teen that it's safe to be honest. Dad must say: "I really want you to answer these questions honestly. I promise to listen without getting defensive, angry, or upset. You don't have to protect me from your honesty."

STEP 2   Split up, find a quiet place, and each write your answers to every question alone. Agree to return in 30 to 45 minutes.

STEP 3   When done, come back together. Agree on how much time you'll take to share your answers. I suggest at least 30 minutes. If possible, leave it open-ended.

STEP 4   Dad shares his answer to Question #1. Teen shares his or her answer to Question #1. Continue alternating responses to each question, in order, until finished. Remember, focus on what's being said, not what you want to say. Use good body language. Don't interrupt or ask too many questions. Avoid getting defensive.

Questions

ABOUT OUR LIVES...

1. Two qualities I like about myself...

2. What I love and respect about you is...

3. If I could change one thing about myself (a quality, physical attribute, attitude, etc.), I would change...

4. Lately, something that's been going well at school (or work) is...

5. If I could do one day over again at school (or work) it would be...

6. I have recently felt worried or stressed-out about...

7. I think you have been worried or stressed-out about...

8. A friend who is very important to me these days is _____ because...

9. Recently, something my friends talk about a lot is...

10. Something happening in the world today (current events) that I think about a lot is...

11. A small change in my life (a new routine, physical growth, new teacher/coach, a driver's license, etc.) that has affected me is...

12. A big change in my life (birth/death, family life, a move, work situation, friendship, health issue, etc.) that has affected me is...

13. FOR TEEN: Dad, when you were my age, how did you handle...
    FOR DAD: When I was your age, things that made my life great were...and things that made it challenging were...

ABOUT OUR RELATIONSHIP...

14. Positive qualities I bring to our relationship are...

15. Positive qualities you bring to our relationship are...

16. Something I really enjoy doing with you is...

17. One of the best things you've done for me lately is...

18. A way I think we're very similar is...

19. A way I think we're different is...

20. Ways that I sometimes make our relationship difficult are...

21. Ways that you sometimes make our relationship difficult are...

22. One way you can strengthen our relationship is...

23. One way that I can strengthen our relationship is...

24. FOR TEEN: Something I've always wondered about our family is...

FOR DAD: Something about my family life I enjoyed growing up and something that was challenging...

25. A subject I find difficult to talk about with you is...

26. A subject I think you find difficult to talk about with me is...

27. An apology I've wanted to make to you is...

28. One of my greatest fears is...

29. I think one of your greatest fears is...

30. Something I need more of (e.g., time, help, respect) from you is...

31. Something I think you need more of from me is...

32. If today were our last day together, one thing I would want to make sure you know is...

33. In the next six months, I want us to...

Acknowledgments

Thank you first to the modern dads and their families for so generously and honestly sharing their stories. I would also like to thank the following people for their inspiration, generosity, time, patience, belief, and support along the way:

Jason Gardner and Mimi Kusch and everyone at New World Library.

Lorin Rees, my agent and dear friend of more than thirty years.

John Aldrich, Haji Shearer, Jim Sullivan, Jonah Matranga, Aaron Kenedi, John Carr, Hannah Matranga, Ann Matranga, John Scully, Greg Pulier, Tara McVicar, Ed Dockray, Korki Aldrich, Monica Sullivan, Jon and Amy Charney.

Jackson Katz, Juan Carlos Arean, Lonna Davis, Mike Nakkula, bell hooks, Craig Norberg-Bohm, Terry Real, Belinda Berman, Lisa Merlo-Booth, Jan Bergstrom, Susan Brady, Caroline Blackwell, Carla and Michael Young, Brad Gioia, Vince Durnan, Sam Cuddeback, Brewster Ely, Tamara Monosoff, Brad Kofed, Shari Santos, Joe and Ellen Vitka, Nancy and Joel Aronie, Melissa Price, Christina and Tim Weir, Leiana Kinnicutt, Craig Keefe, Richard Claytor, Marylin Lasky, Rich Batten, Joe Caronna, Rob Berkeley, Greg O'Melia, Michael Brosnan, Ross Browner, Jim Cooper, David Ingram, Joe Laferrera, Bill Burke, Frank Steel, Michael Thompson, Jean Kilbourne, Sandee Mirell, and John Longo.

Diane and David Jensen, Peter Badalament, Kelli Birtwell, Daniel Jensen, and Tony Badalament. Jack and Alberta Ellis, Peter Donlin, and our many loved ones from Michigan, Ohio, and New York.

This book would not exist if it were not for my wife, Katie's, grace, patience, tolerance, beauty, and strength of body, spirit, and soul. And thank you, of course, to my two wonderful children, Stella and Jake, for their endless love and support throughout this journey.

Notes

Chapter 1. Create Your Own Vision

1. Terry Real, *Relational Parenting: Raising Healthy Boys and Girls*, compact disc, Relational Life Institute, 2006.

Chapter 2. Be the Bridge between Your Past and Your Future

1. *All Men Are Sons: Exploring the Legacy of Fatherhood*, directed by John Badalament and produced by John Badalament and Chad Grochowski, Boxtop Studios, 2006.
2. Pia Mellody, *The Intimacy Factor: The Ground Rules for Overcoming the Obstacles to Truth, Respect, and Lasting Love* (HarperCollins, 2003).
3. As quoted in John Bradshaw, *Family Secrets: The Path to Self-Acceptance and Reunion* (Bantam, 1996), 264.
4. B.M. Groves, *Children Who See Too Much: Lessons from the Child Witness to Violence Project* (Beacon Press, 2002).

Chapter 3. Be a New Kind of Provider

1. Families and Work Institute, "Times Are Changing: Gender and Generation at Work and at Home," 2009. Available at www.census.gov/population/www/socdemo/hh-fam/cps2007.html

2. Stephanie Coontz, *The Way We Never Were: American Families and the Nostalgia Trap* (Basic Books, 1992; from new introduction, 2000), xx.

3. Human Rights and Equal Opportunity Commission, "Submission to the Inquiry into Child Custody Arrangements in the Event of Family Separation," 2003, 18.

4. U.S. Department of Labor, "The American Time Use Survey," Bureau of Labor Statistics, 2005.

5. Anita Haataja, "Fathers' Use of Paternity and Parental Leave in the Nordic Countries" (Helsinki: The Social Insurance Institution, Research Department, 2009). Available at www.kela.fi/research (accessed 12/1/09).

6. Testimony from Ellen Galinsky, Parents Raising Children: The Workplace. U.S. Senate Health, Education, Labor, and Pensions Committee Subcommittee on Children and Families, 2004.

Chapter 4. Find Balance through Ritual

1. Work and Family Institute, "U.S. Workforce Addressing Issues of Life On and Off the Job."

2. Terry Real, *I Don't Want to Talk about It: Overcoming the Secret Legacy of Male Depression* (Fireside, 1997).

Chapter 5. Know Your Children

1. Ricky Pelach-Galil, "The Re-creation of the Father by His Adolescent Son" (PhD diss., Hebrew University of Jerusalem, 2003).

2. Linda Nielsen, "Fathers and Daughters: A Needed Course in Family Studies," *Marriage and Family Review* 38 (2005): 1–15. Available at www.wfu.edu/~nielsen.

3. N. Lezin, L. Rolleri, S. Bean, and J. Taylor, *Parent-Child Connectedness: Implications for Research, Interventions, and Positive Impacts on Adolescent Health* (Santa Cruz, CA: ETR Associates, 2004), 49.

4. Kahlil Gibran, *The Prophet* (New York: Knopf, 1985), 17.

5. Michael S. Kimmel, "Gender Equality: Not for Women Only," International Women's Day Seminar, European Parliament, Brussels, March 8, 2001.

6.   C. W. Nord and J. West, *Fathers' and Mothers' Involvement in Their Children's Schools by Family Type and Resident Status*. U.S. Department of Education, National Center for Education Statistics, 2001.

7.   bell hooks, *The Will to Change: Men, Masculinity, and Love* (New York: Atria Books, 2004).

Chapter 6. Be Known by Your Children

1.   John Gottman, with Joan Declaire, *Raising an Emotionally Intelligent Child* (Simon & Schuster, 1998).

2.   Kathleen Mullan Harris, "The National Longitudinal Study of Adolescent Health, Waves I and II, 1994–1996; Wave III, 2001–2002; Wave IV, 2007–2009" (Chapel Hill, NC: Carolina Population Center, 2009).

3.   Kyle Puett, *Fatherneed: Why Father Care Is as Essential as Mother Care for Your Child* (Broadway, 2001).

4.   Mark Gerzon, *A Choice of Heroes: The Changing Face of American Manhood* (Houghton-Mifflin, 1992).

Conclusion

1.   Dr. Eli Newberger, *The Men They Will Become: The Nature and Nurture of Male Character* (Perseus, 1999).

Index

229

About the Author

John Badalament, EdM, is a writer, filmmaker, international speaker, and leader in the fatherhood field. A graduate of Harvard's Graduate School of Education, John consults with schools, parent groups, mental health professionals, corrections facilities, and religious groups. John's work has been featured on NPR and in *Men's Health* magazine, the *Los Angeles Times*, the *Rocky Mountain News*, and *National PTA* magazine. In 2007, he was recognized in the *New York Times* by the Family Violence Prevention Fund's Founding Fathers campaign to end violence against women and children. *All Men Are Sons: Exploring the Legacy of Fatherhood*, his acclaimed documentary film, aired on PBS stations across America. His most recent film project is entitled *Gender Traps: How Marriage Problems Start in Kindergarten*. John lives with his wife and two kids in Massachusetts.

For more info, visit his website: www.moderndads.net

NEW WORLD LIBRARY is dedicated to publishing books and other media that inspire and challenge us to improve the quality of our lives and the world.

We are a socially and environmentally aware company, and we strive to embody the ideals presented in our publications. We recognize that we have an ethical responsibility to our customers, our staff members, and our planet.

We serve our customers by creating the finest publications possible on personal growth, creativity, spirituality, wellness, and other areas of emerging importance. We serve New World Library employees with generous benefits, significant profit sharing, and constant encouragement to pursue their most expansive dreams.

As a member of the Green Press Initiative, we print an increasing number of books with soy-based ink on 100 percent postconsumer-waste recycled paper. Also, we power our offices with solar energy and contribute to nonprofit organizations working to make the world a better place for us all.

Our products are available
in bookstores everywhere.
For our catalog, please contact:

New World Library
14 Pamaron Way
Novato, California 94949

Phone: 415-884-2100 or 800-972-6657
Catalog requests: Ext. 50
Orders: Ext. 52
Fax: 415-884-2199
Email: escort@newworldlibrary.com

To subscribe to our electronic newsletter, visit
www.newworldlibrary.com

HELPING TO PRESERVE OUR ENVIRONMENT

7,205 trees were saved

New World Library uses 100% postconsumer-waste recycled paper for our books whenever possible, even if it costs more. During 2009 this choice saved the following precious resources:

www.newworldlibrary.com

ENERGY	WASTEWATER	GREENHOUSE GASES	SOLID WASTE
22 MILLION BTU	3 MILLION GAL.	685,000 LB.	200,000 LB.

Environmental impact estimates were made using the Environmental Defense Fund Paper Calculator @ www.papercalculator.org.